"As the CEO of a mortuary and memorial park many grief recovery books cross my desk each year. All too often these books contain essential information but the presentation is imposing and esoteric. *The Healing Power of Grief* is written in every day language and in an easy to understand format. The anecdotes are real life and relate to all who are in the successive stages of the grieving process. The workbook exercises are clear, helpful and direct the participant with meaningful topics. I would be proud to have this book in our library." **Mark Friedman, CEO, Hillside Memorial Park and Mortuary**

"With insight and compassion, the authors lead readers through their grief and into a healed future of purpose and joy. For the bereaved, their family and friends who don't know where to turn, these are the pages to turn to." **Eleanore Osborne, Daytona Beach News-Journal**

"The authors do a magnificent job of guiding the reader through grief, in both its emotional and pragmatic sense. This comprehensive book, which provides space for journaling one's recovery, will undoubtedly be an enormous asset to the field of grief recover for years to come." **Pamela D. Blair, Ph.D., psychotherapist, author of *The Next Fifty Years: A Guide for Women at Midlife and Beyond*, co-author of *I Wasn't Ready to Say Goodbye***

'*The Healing Power of Grief* is a poignant reminder that our loved ones are with us - always!" **Dougall Fraser, *But You Knew That Already : What a Psychic Can Teach You About Life*** (Rodale) www.DougallFraser.com

The Healing Power of Grief

The Healing Power of Grief

The Journey Through Loss
to Life and Laughter

*Gloria Lintermans
and Dr. Marilyn Stolzman*

CHAMPION PRESS, LTD.
WISCONSIN

ALSO BY THE AUTHORS:
The Healing Power of Love

CHAMPION PRESS, LTD.
BELGIUM, WISCONSIN
Copyright © 2006 Gloria Lintermans and Dr. Marilyn Stolzman

ISBN: 1932783482
LCCN: 2005937786

Manufactured in the United States of America

10 9 8 7 6 5 4 3 2 1

In memory of my precious late husband
Rick
Gloria Lintermans

Dedicated to the courageous members, past and present, of the H.O.P.E. Unit Foundation for Bereavement, Loss and Transition who have attended this program in order to help themselves and each other to heal and to the memory of my beloved parents, my mother Lillian, who intuitively understood the power of love, and my father William, for his gift of words and his ability to "speak the King's English."

Marilyn Stolzman, Ph.D., L.M.F.T.

Acknowledgements

THIS BOOK WOULD not have been possible without the unflagging encouragement and wonderful guidance of the following individuals. To my first best friend, my dear sister Marsha for your loving and generous heart, for celebrating my triumphs while offering extraordinary comfort in my pain. To Hal, for your unquestioning belief in this project and my ability to pull it off, and for your unique ability to have invited joy back into my life.

To Marjie, Linda, Gail, and my dear parents for your loving ability to provide a safe place during my grieving, healing, and sometimes pain-filled memories while writing this book. To my agent, Sharlene Martin, who, if not for your energy, tenacity and consciously acquired understanding of our subject, this book would not have come to light. To Brook Noel and Sara Pattow of Champion Press for your determination to "heal" the world, one book at a time.

My gratitude to Bill, Carole, Clare, Clark, Doug, Francine, Hal, Geri, Jeanette, Joette, Laura, Marjanie, Martha, Nancy, Rebecca, Robert, Ruthe, Sherry, Sonia, Steve, Sue, widows and widowers who so generously shared their stories of pain and hope so that others may benefit.

To Richard, Amy, Evan, Lauren and Stacy, my love and gratitude for your encouragement and support during times of pain and times of joy. To Ellie, my dear friend for reading this manuscript and offering suggestions that were always right on the mark.

To Dr. Jo Christner, Psy.D. for your willingness to share your knowledge and professional experience, thank you for your important contribution and generous heart. And lastly, my gratitude goes to my co-author, Dr. Marilyn Stolzman and H.O.P.E., for your knowledge and my healing – for without both, this book would never have been possible.

Gloria Lintermans

I WOULD LIKE TO thank our agent Sharlene Martin for believing in us. My thanks to Brook Noel for her wise and valuable editorial advice, and to Sara Pattow of Champion Press for your support. To my daughters Dana and Rachel for your constant love and encouragement to write; to Auntie, who understood instinctively how to stand by the dying with love and compassion; and, to my staff at H.O.P.E. Unit Foundation; Marsha Ambraziunas, M.A., M.F.T., Bonnie Ban, M.A., M.F.T., Erin Childs, M.A., M.F.T., Jo Christner, Psy.D., M.F.T., Cass Lyons, M.A.,M.F.T., Natalie Taback, M.A., M.F.T., and Dayna Vainstein, M.A., M.F.T. for your dedication and hard work, and to Bob who listened, reflected and provided a sounding board for my thoughts. You encouraged me to tell this story.

I would also like to thank the bereaved who remained anonymous but shared their stories to enrich our book.

My gratitude goes to the current Board of Directors of the H.O.P.E. Unit Foundation for Bereavement, Loss and Hope: Chief Financial Officer, George Lippert, C.P.A.; Vice President Leonard Kaneg; Vice President

Leib Lehmann, Ph.D.; Vice President Jerry Watterson; Recording Secretary; Bill Frankenstein, C.F.P.; Mark Friedman, CEO Hillside Memorial Park and Mortuary; Judy Geller; Stephanie Crane Hirsh; Gerry Moscowitz; Advisors to the Board, Joe McNair, Ph.D., Creative Living Center; Mary Louise Ozohan, M.D., Valley Radiation Oncology Center; Rabbi Harold Schulweis,Valley Beth Shalom; and, Chic Wolk for their hard work, support and encouragement and for believing in H.O.P.E.

To Jo Christner, Psy.D. valued friend and colleague, who always goes the extra mile and has such a caring heart.

To Stephan David Hewitt, my friend, who provided wise counsel as a sounding board and for his supportive work with H.O.P.E.

To Phyllis Goldberg for your friendship, love and care, Gloria Simons for your love, support, encouragement, friendship and special light.

To my dear friend and co-author Gloria Lintermans, I thank you for your patience at my limited technical knowledge, your up-lifting attitude to get the work done, and your smiling persistence for completion.

Marilyn Stolzman, Ph.D., L.M.F.T.

Grief Is a Passage

The management of grief is, in essence,
the management of self.
Grief is a passage, a lonely pilgrimage.
It is a birthday process where
we are reborn into new identity,
new life, and new hope.
As in our first birth, *we have no choice.*
Author Unknown

CONTENTS

THE HEALING POWER OF THOUGHT WORKBOOK

INTRODUCTION

New York City, September 11, 2001
3,000 dead

Southern Asia, earthquake and tsunami, December, 2004
162,000 dead

Middle East conflict
2,000+ dead and counting

Atlantic Hurricanes Katrina & Rita, September 2005
1,000+ dead

Northern Pakistan, earthquake, October, 2005
79,000 dead

Throughout America
15+ million widows and widowers.

Some of the most widespread beliefs about mourning are largely myths, new scientific findings are showing. And researchers warn that these myths can increase the mourners' distress by holding them to false expectations of what is "normal." *"New Studies Find Many Myths About Mourning" by Daniel Goleman, Ph.D. and author of Emotional Intelligence (Bantam Books, 1995)*

As the saying goes, there are only two things unavoidable in life: taxes and dying. Along with dying there is, more often than not, a spouse or life-partner left to grieve. These bereft partners are our concern. Why are some able to heal and eventually experience a fulfilling new life, while others wither emotionally, spiritually, and even physically, never fully recovering from their loss? When losing a spouse is so common, why do we need a blueprint to overcome our suffering and eventually, achieve healing? Why is *healthy* mourning, as opposed to a prolonged state of emotional denial, important in creating a rewarding new life?

The Healing Power of Grief is Gloria Lintermans' story, twenty-four months of mourning and healing following the death of her precious husband, Rick. It is also Dr. Marilyn Stolzman's vision, a psychotherapist who specializes in grief counseling, offering tools, not psychobabble, a blueprint as it were, to help you to face your loss, mourn, and eventually, heal.

Together, we share our experiences as we take you gently by the hand, to give you comfort and direction during this confusing and painful time. It has been shown that the *only* way to arrive at a healthy, *healed* integration, adjustment and transition is by going through the shock, denial, envy, anger, depression, and guilt that the loss of a spouse predictably inspires. It is important to note that these stages are based loosely on the "stages of grief" first acknowledged by Dr. Elizabeth Kubler-Ross for those "living while dying."

Unlike any other book, *The Healing Power of Grief* is based on the *Time Sequences of Grief*. Each chapter represents a time sequence of mourning divided by months. Each include a first-hand account of mourning; answers to commonly asked questions concerning your day-to-day life, ie., questions you might be asking yourself; Dr. Stolzman's reassuring explanation of what you are feeling in keeping with that time frame; and, a roadmap of helpful Do's and Don'ts to guide you and your support community on your path to recovery.

There is no way *around* grief. You can't hide from it (for long anyway) or run away from it – it follows wherever you go. Losing a spouse can be especially challenging because you are deprived not only of your *day-to-day life*, but also, your *couple future*. Contrary to the old adage, time alone, (unfortunately) does not heal anything. A 1983 Harvard study of widows and widowers found that 40 percent were still anxious and depressed as long as four years after the death of their spouse. Real healing is a combination of time and *educated grieving* that truly allows you to embrace not only the continuation of your life, but the joy that life offers.

We offer healing strategies, while also acknowledging shifting, overlapping feelings, as you overcome helplessness and immobility and move forward, at your own speed, along with specifics on creating a more balanced life, including its many and varied aspects: growth, spirituality, recreation, health and exercise, community, career, family, and financially security. We also recognize the need for social interaction and exchange, such as being part of a larger community, not grieving alone, and developing a partnership with the world.

We will help you to know appropriate things to say to take care of yourself, how to handle unintentionally hurtful comments that may come from friends and pointers on dealing with holidays, difficult days, and special occasions. We offer comfort while recognizing the importance of forgiveness and the return to a life that embraces loving. We include tools for embracing a giving heart, finding courage at the darkest times, being open to joy, and trusting others. We offer coping strategies, while also recognizing that everyone is different. How we grieve is affected by our personality, intellect, sense of humor, past experience with loss, and social, cultural, ethnic, and religious backgrounds – and so we provide tools that are flexible and adaptable.

We recognize the presence of stresses in the mourners' life, and on the positive side, we recognize the ways in which your beliefs, spiritual sense, and support systems all contribute to the grieving and healing process. And, we will examine the meaning of individual loss, the role that the deceased filled in the family, and the unfinished business between you and your loved one.

Specifically, we have strived to offer answers and coping strategies for your greatest and lesser concerns, such as: *What am I going to do with the rest of my life? Does this feeling of numbness get better? Will I be able to travel alone and take care of myself? Will I be afraid forever? When I get sick, how will I manage? When should I discard my spouse's clothing? When should I stop wearing my wedding ring?*

And more: *Why haven't I been able to cry yet? Why am I afraid to leave my house when I used to be active? Or, Why am I "running" all the time? How can I stop myself from breaking down in tears in very embarrassing places? How should I talk about this to my young/grown kids? I hate feeling so dependent on others, and wonder...Will I ever feel capable again? How can I deal with the first birthday, anniversary and holiday after losing my spouse?*

And still more: *Why do I feel guilty about being happy again? Why do I feel disloyal to my deceased spouse about wanting to date again? I've been told that the one-year mark ends the mourning time, but I don't feel that way. In fact, I feel worse than at the beginning. Why? What future is there for me beyond the feeling of unending, unchanging desolation? How will I know when I'm ready to date? When is it too soon? Am I forgetting my spouse if I begin dating? What will my children say? Why am I hesitating and troubled by uncertainty? Am I going to spend the rest of my life lonely, feeling like a "fifth wheel" with our old couple-friends? How can I have any kind of social life? Will I ever be able to remember the joys, hopes, memories ... smiles ... without feeling sadness? Or, My husband was abusive to me and we had a horrible marriage. Why am I mourning?*

We offer direction and support information for those mourning from non-traditional relationships, such as the gay, lesbian, bisexual and transgender communities, as well as heterosexual life-partners.

While grieving is similar to all, we liken the experience to many people in the same water, however, each in different boats with a unique set of oars. To that end, you will find many stories from widows and widowers throughout this book, including Gloria's.

You will also note that various "Do's and Don'ts" for yourself and your support community are sometimes repeated in several chapters. This is not in error but a deliberate reminder that mourning is a back-and-forth experience and many feelings *will* repeat during this two-year time period.

The RESOURCES section lists organizations, publications, support groups, and Internet sites for additional information and/or finding a bereavement support group. The advantage of joining such a group lies in its feedback and continual sharing. David Spiegel author of *Living Beyond the Limits: New Hope and Help for Facing Life-Threatening Illness,* (Crown) states that members of support groups do 50 percent better in their grief recovery.

Additionally, we will touch briefly on how young children grieve as caring for children may be a necessary part of your own recovery.

Lastly, *The Healing Power of Thought,* a companion workbook, gives you a place to store your grief outside of yourself so that painful feelings can be expressed and eventually released. Writing your thoughts down also provides you with a record as you mourn your late spouse so that you can look back over your journey and take comfort in your progress.

The hard reality is that the only way *OVER* this loss, is to be willing to go *THROUGH* the pain of mourning. We want to help. And so, let's begin ...

Mourner's Bill of Rights

We have the right to express our grieving in our own way.

We have the right to know that grieving is slow, hard work, and to move through it at our own pace.

We have the right to express our feelings about grief and to explore them.

We have the right to forgive ourselves for the things we think we "should" have done or "might" have done and realize that what we did in that moment of time was based on the information at hand and that we did the best that we could with the knowledge we had.

We have the right to be ourselves and to recognize our strengths and our limitations.

We have the right to participate actively in our mourning, to remember the past with fond memories and to allow ourselves to enjoy our lives again.

We have the right to move forward and to speak of our pain, whether that makes people uncomfortable or not.

We have the right to go back and forth in our grieving; some days making progress and other days slipping back.

We have the right to express our emotions and to have others bear witness to our story

We have the right to believe that we will have a whole life again!

Marilyn Stolzman, Ph.D., L.M.F.T

THE HEALING POWER OF GRIEF   8

Grieving Is ...

Needing someone to tell you how special your loved one is to you.

Not wanting to forget that "specialness," shared joys and happiness.

Getting to know more of yourself and your loved one by seeing them with new vision and understanding them in new ways.

Feeling that you might rip from pain, which you may never recover from or feel whole again.

Feeling like, "My god, how can I continue?" and "How much more can I take?"

Feeling like you have wasted so much time and could have had so much more.

Feeling that you didn't do enough and didn't understand what could have been done.

Feeling that you've been left alone.

Feeling angry, feeling no justice, rhyme or reason.

Being mad that you weren't given the opportunity to say what you wanted to say.

Being upset that your loved one didn't allow you to help more.

Remembering joys, hopes, dates, memories, caresses, smiles, words, and feelings.

Knowing that no one will understand your grief the way that you do.

Growth, movement, and learning.

Good.

Loving.

Shanti Project
Reprinted with permission

1.

The Five Time
Sequences of Healing Grief

WHILE EVERYONE EXPERIENCES grief and mourning in his or her own way and time, predictably there are *time sequences* and emotions common to all. You may find yourself going through each of the emotional stages of shock, denial, anger, depression, and finally, integration, adjustment and transition in the order we have listed, or you may find yourself jumping all over the place in a forward-and-backward movement.

You may seem to skip one stage completely, only to encounter it long after you have thought yourself emotionally healed. How so? You may not have allowed yourself to recognize, for instance, anger directed inward, or directed outward toward your late spouse or even the world-at-large until you are feeling stronger and in control of your life once again.

You may even go through some of these steps more than once and experience even deeper feelings each successive time. Or, in the course of any one day, you may find yourself in touch with all of these stages. Mourning is not an exact process; it is loose and fluid and does not fit into a cookie-cutter mold. We encourage you to use this information as *your* process dictates by reading whichever chapter or stage that explores what you are feeling right now, regardless of time.

Each chapter opens with Gloria's story, illustrating the daily concerns that the bereaved express during this *time sequence*; our pains, hopes, joys, feelings of sadness, hopelessness, shifts, changes, the slow process of recovery, and healing.

The second half of each chapter explores the corresponding *emotional stage* of the grieving process and the symptoms associated with each.

During our two year time frame, we will look at and deal with what mourning is emotionally, the issues that come up, thoughts associated with these emotions, the struggles of daily living, and the questions of appropriateness.

"Do's and Don'ts" for the mourner and your support community found at the end of each chapter offer practical ways for dealing successfully, on a day-to-day basis, with mourning before you move along to the next *time sequence*.

"When confronted with the loss of a spouse," says Dr. Jo Christner, Psy.D., a licensed Psychologist and Marriage, Family Therapist in private practice and who has facilitated weekly spousal-loss groups in Los Angeles for over 13 years, "we are suddenly thrown into a difficult, lonely journey of grief. It's not a journey that we want and often don't know how to maneuver. Although psychology has identified the stages of grief (**shock, denial, anger, depression,** and **integration/adjustment/transition**) many factors make it a unique, individual struggle, not exactly like anyone else's.

"As you go through the grief stages, you will be challenged to move through the "world in-between," the transitional place between an ending and a beginning. You might be thinking 'this must be a mistake. I'm not supposed to be here. It no longer feels like my world.' Everything is changed. The life that you once knew is gone. Life no longer seems familiar or comfortable. It can be confusing, painful and disorienting. It's the place that must be visited between loss and beginning a changed life, between feeling hopeless and finding hope, between re-identifying and reinventing. It's the place of healing through grief and learning to integrate your world that has changed forever. It will never again be the same ... but you will begin again.

"As you go through the stages of grief, you will begin to find light and to heal. It's normal to have loss. It's normal to grieve. It's normal to begin again. That is the way of life. May the following suggestions help you through the process of grief, transition and, healing.

1. Talk to yourself in a way that perpetuates healing. Keep your thoughts in the present moment. It's too easy to feel hopeless and predict the worst by thinking into the future. The future's not here yet ... and you will change. Determining what the future holds will only reflect the pain that you feel now.

2. Have a "linking" object, something that belonged to your loved one (i.e. ring, shirt, socks, picture, keychain). It can bring comfort during a time when nothing seems to bring comfort. It's ok to carry it, touch it and remember. It will help you to grieve.

3. Read books and inspirational thoughts which educate, support and bring you comfort.

4. Believe that you can survive this loss and heal. Grieving is an individual journey. Trust that you will heal ... in your own unique way.

5. Seek support through friends, family and support groups. Isolation only increases your loneliness. Being in a support group with others who are grieving can give you comfort and reassurance. My favorite saying is: "We're not on this earth to see through one another. We're here to see one another through."

6. Give yourself the time that you need to grieve and to heal. Sometimes you need to 're-visit' the grief. Sometimes you need to 're-visit' the distractions and resources in your life. Allow room for both. It's the "space" in between where the healing occurs.

7. If your grief is complicated, seek professional help from a licensed therapist.

"Grieving is a process, not an event. Psychology believes that healthy, uncomplicated grief for a spouse takes approximately two years. For some individuals, it will be shorter and for others, longer. Trust YOUR process and your journey. Trust that you, too, will heal. Trust that you will find life and light again," reassures Dr. Christner.

2.

Time Sequences of Healing Grief
The First Four Months
Shock

ON MAY 22ND AT 2:20 *in the morning my husband died. As I was sleeping in an armchair by his side in the hospital, his nurse gently woke me with the words, "He's gone." Reaching over, I put my hand on his arm, stunned by the coldness of his skin. As my world shattered into a million fragmented pieces, I softly sobbed, my head falling slowly until it rested next to his on his hospital bed. After a devastating battle of two and a half years, the ups and downs of fighting disease, his body had finally given out. The fight was gone; we'd lost the war.*

My sister, who had traveled from the east coast, had been by my side in the hospital during these final weeks. Sensing my need to be alone for the last time with my precious husband, she tiptoed out of the room to make whatever arrangements were necessary at the nursing station.

After a while, the nurse explained that she needed to prepare the body for transfer to the mortuary. Body?! Rick was now a "body." A few minutes before, he'd been a person. My sister walked out to the parking lot with me, her arm around my waist for support. I was physically and emotionally exhausted. As we reached the hospital parking lot, the warm Southern California sun began to rise, yet I felt cold, a chill I was afraid would never go away. We drove home. All I wanted to do was sleep, yet I could only weep.

In the blink of an eye, my world was completely out of step, or I was completely out of step with the world. I felt totally disconnected to anything but my sadness. Once home, I heard the phone ring, but wouldn't answer it. My family offered food, but eating was out of the question.

I needed to decide what Rick would be wearing for burial. Although he'd lost 60 pounds from his 6'2," 200+ frame during his illness and nothing fit properly, I still chose the suit he wore when we were married, his favorite tie, and bedroom slippers so that his feet would be comfortable.

The next day my son, sister, Rick's two daughters and I went to the mortuary to choose the casket. As I stood in front of the selection, tears ran down my face. I couldn't believe that what was happening was real; it felt like such a horrible dream. My family gathered around me, wanting to comfort me, to take the sadness away. Nothing helped. Finally I made a selection and we met with the mortuary director to complete the paperwork. Did I want the body embalmed? No! And no makeup! And a closed casket! After all the suffering my husband had endured during his illness, the tests, the surgeries, the pain, I didn't want to subject him to anything further. I was numb, yet angry, all at the same time. But who was I angry at?

The funeral is a blur; I had only enough energy to weep. Thinking to offer consolation, people would say: "Take comfort that he's no longer in pain." I would nod, all the while thinking to myself, but he's gone and that's worse! Time and time again I found myself in the position of having to take care of peripheral friends who thought they were taking care of me, but I kept my rage to myself.

As they should, in time, my family had to get back to their own lives. My sister returned to the east coast, all the while saying, "If you need me to stay longer or to come back, just let me know." She wanted to take care of me and would have stayed as long as I asked her to, but I knew somewhere in all my numbness that no matter how long she was there, this was a pain I had to deal with alone and, on some emotional level, I think I believed that if everyone around me got back to their own lives, so would I. But what I hadn't considered was that my life was now irrevocably changed, my day-to-day life and my couple future.

Trying to take care of what needed to be done was exhausting. I felt confused, nothing felt real. Going through Rick's belongings was something I couldn't even think about, much less do. I had lived alone years before we met, but found the darkness of night took away any defense I had against the overwhelming sadness. For weeks I slept with lights on all over the house. Yet, no matter how much I slept, I never felt rested. A debilitating weariness was ongoing. I joined a weekly bereavement support group, not really knowing why, sensing it was something I needed to do. As one day melted into the next, I had no protection from my sadness or the feelings of disconnect from the world I'd known.

Common Questions

Will the pain ever go away? Will I feel better?

Why haven't I been able to cry yet?

Why am I afraid to leave my house when I used to be active?

Why am I running all the time, filling every waking moment with frantic activity?

Why do I find it impossible to accomplish even simple tasks, or even get out of bed?

Why do I find myself breaking down in embarrassing places? Why can't I have any control over my emotions?

Why don't I have an appetite? Or, why can't I stop eating?

Nothing makes sense. Am I going crazy?

Why am I so forgetful?

When I have the energy, how do I set new goals?

How do I even begin to know what I want?

What am I going to do with the rest of my life? Does this feeling of numbness get better?

I'm not used to traveling alone and taking care of myself. Will I be afraid forever?

When I get sick, how will I take care of myself?

When should I discard my spouse's clothing? When should I stop wearing my wedding ring?

How should I talk about this to my young/grown kids?

I hate feeling so dependent on others; will I ever feel capable again?

How can I deal with the first birthday, anniversary and holiday after losing my spouse?

What future is there for me beyond the feeling of unending, unchanging desolation?

How will I know when I'm ready to date? When is it too soon?

Am I forgetting my spouse if I begin dating? What will my children say? Why am I hesitating and troubled by uncertainty?

Am I going to spend the rest of my life lonely? Feeling like a fifth wheel with our old couple-friends, how can I have any kind of social life?

Will I ever be able to remember the joys, hopes, memories ... smiles ... without feeling sadness?

FACING YOUR LOSS head on is difficult because loving is all-encompassing; love took most of your emotional energy as you embraced your spouse. We cared that they were fulfilled and well. We wanted to protect them and make them happy. We were devoted, so much so, that losing this loved one, felt crippling. And so, when they are gone, we need to learn how to transform this energy into something positive. Not a "substitute," but a conversion from a "we" to an "I." Not in a selfish manner, but as a way of refocusing, we ask "How do I live my life in a positive way without you ... not losing the memory and loving feelings of you, but incorporating them and going on? What tools can I find? How do I learn to heal in a way that's positive and energizing instead of depleting?"

Grieving is a process that unfolds during the 24 months after the death of your spouse. At the beginning of your mourning, it is not uncommon to have limitless questions with answers that feel completely out of reach.

Yet, despite the overwhelming pain, you instinctually know, somewhere deep within your heart that: "I need to stay alive, alive in a way that supports me *and* the "us" that was. I must seek a new emergence of myself after visiting the 'dark.' I sense that this awareness comes from the realm of my feelings, not from the sphere of my thinking." This is your beginning, to mourn and to heal.

Disaster looks us in the face and we survive. We hardly know how we do that, but we succeed. Underneath all the pain, there are elements of faith and trust, an "I can't lose" feeling, and the energy to go on and survive.

Beginning to Mourn
The earliest feelings of mourning include the initial shock (this can't be happening), the denial of the reality, and feeling overwhelmed and numb. It is not uncommon to feel some loss of self-esteem and extreme vulnerability. Symptoms usually include a variety of internal complaints, a great deal of crying, insomnia, waking from sleep or not being able to fall asleep, feeling anxious, loss of appetite, possible sweaty hands and heart palpitations. You may also experience irritability, lack of patience, forgetfulness,

distractibility and loss of concentration. Feelings of sadness and loneliness accompany feeling bewilderment. Disassociation of feeling is common. "I feel split off and distracted; I'm not there." Or, "I feel like I'm on 'automatic pilot.'" These feelings are normal. It is important to develop the ability to self-nurture during this most stressful time. On the Holmes and Rahe Social Readjustment Rating Scale, death of a spouse ranks at 100 percent as a stressor.

Concentrate on self-care and physical check-ups, appropriate nutrition, rest and exercise. Talk honestly of what you are feeling to friends and family. Feelings are not right or wrong; whatever you are feeling is appropriate. Acknowledge that there is no "script" to follow and know that talking about your feelings to understanding family and friends is good, yet be aware that no one understands grieving until it is their experience.

Living through the Pain

The temptation now is to go to denial. Your loss will be with you 24 hours a day as you traverse this bewildering early time sequence. You may feel "frozen," "locked up," emotionally numb, scared and more capable of crying than talking. You may find it hard to be coherent or put two sentences together. You may want to go into some dark corner and scream. You are searching for tools while feeling half crazy. You want gentleness and support but are often quick to anger and anger often spills out everywhere. Being able to focus is impossible. Feeling scattered and out of sorts is your new norm.

With your loss, you feel as if you are on the wrong road or out of your familiar community, or as one mourner expressed, "I'm living in the wrong neighborhood." Vaguely, the house looks familiar, but the world is strange and un-kempt. Nothing feels right. Anything and everything your friends and family say can feel irritating. There is no place to go that is comfortable. You are not at home in your body; there is no good place to be, anywhere.

Grieving is exhausting. Feeling tired emotionally is draining. If you are lucky enough to be able to exercise, this can be some outlet for your inner tension.

Sleeping can be uncomfortable. You might fall asleep and quickly wake up, or want to sleep all the time. Internally, you can feel very empty and want to fill up, often by overeating. On the other hand, there may be loss of appetite and you can't eat at all. Either way, there may be extremes of mood. Emotional stability can feel transitory. There may be good moments in a day but they may be overshadowed by, moodiness, despair, internal pain and great sadness.

Day-By-Day Grieving

Hal has this to say: "Well, quite obviously, the first few months were beyond description. There were just horrible moments of despair and loneliness. I was only able to get relief after the first few weeks when the meds that I was taking kicked in, and, after the therapy started to ease some of my feelings of guilt and a bunch of random other feelings that my wife's death brought forth." As the months progressed, Hal's pain eased, but the loneliness persisted. "I think that was probably the most debilitating aspect of mourning, the absence of my mate. She had been there since, really, childhood because we'd known each other since we were 14 years old."

Early bereavement is a slow process. You might expect to make greater progress along these strange roads than you do. Inner patience is important, as is allowing you to feel whatever you feel. At first it feels as if nothing will ever change or get better, but the intensity diminishes in time. The raw and open wound slowly begins to heal. Bad feelings are less frequent and linger for a shorter time.

How do you change a "rotten place" to a place of optimism and hope? How do you move from despair to a lighter meadow? How do you learn to dream again? How do you move to wholeness?

What is the inner process of achieving wisdom? What does the heart advise? How does the heart heal? The following exercise can be helpful:

Envision each chamber of your heart as a separate room.
Envision each chamber filled with sunlight and air.
Envision breezes blowing through.
This room is different from a room with no light. When you are sad you can love the dark and hate the sunlight, but when you allow sunlight in, you can again breathe in that room. Learn to breathe again.

Sainthood

Have you begun to think of your late spouse in terms of perfect? Or, that the relationship was perfect, or as if the achievement of "sainthood" validates your pain? What is gained or meant by this thinking? It enables you to stay emotionally stuck. "Look what I lost." The enormity of the loss can become your sad lament. When the human characteristics of him/her emerge once more, it is often a strong indication that you are getting better. This is one way that the psyche is protected until you are ready to mourn. On the other hand, you may feel sheepish about admitting, even to yourself, that your marriage was less than perfect. Give yourself permission to feel these feelings, knowing you are far from alone.

Often the bereaved, at this stage, attribute sainthood status to their lost loved one. It is a measure of your healing when you are able to remove your deceased spouse's sainthood status.

Humor

The use of humor transcends all the stages of healing and needs to be used and recognized as a wonderful tool for self-balance. Humor keeps our head above water at a time when we think our logic is going to float away and drown us. It offers leverage, relief and distance from pain. There are moments when we think we will never laugh again and then, in the most unexpected moment, there is a smile and it is so welcome. At first, you may feel uncomfortable with laughter, but participating in a bereavement support group will help you to acknowledge not only how good it feels, but how wonderful it is to witness and participate in.

Healing from Within

Your search for your inner guide requires an inner quietness – a place where the brook of energy runs freely – the water flows. The currents swirl, life is not stagnant. Ask yourself the question, What do I want? What feels right and true to me at this moment? When one is overwhelmed by anxiety, natural intuition is blocked – the flow is interrupted.

How can you learn to relax the body when you feel tense? How can you be grounded when you don't feel grounded? One technique is to use breath as an energizing source. Visualize your breath and let go of body tension. Imagine moving into a deep quiet inner space where there is an innate wisdom that spills forward as if it were a waterfall. The water soothes and comforts. Ask God, or the Universe, for guidance and trust the reply that comes from that inner place.

Beginning to Find Answers

Q: *Why are holidays so hard?*
A: Holidays are reminders of family occasions and have, often painful, associations to events and people. They evoke memories, feelings and nostalgia for what was. It is helpful to do things in a different way at holiday time and to make plans to be with family or friends rather than being alone.

Q: *My husband and I had a troubled relationship. Why am I still grieving so much?*

A: Even in a difficult relationship, people grieve. We often grieve the loss of a relationship that didn't have resolution. Any chance to redeem the relationship is gone, and that is another type of loss. We have many feelings about lost opportunities, regrets and what might have been. It is normal to be sad, even if the relationship was a troubled one.

Q: *I'm frightened of being alone. How do I deal with that as I grieve?*

A: There are two aspects to this question. First, there is a difference between being "lonely" and "alone." Most people have trouble tolerating their own "aloneness" within the bereavement experience. And so, they attend one activity after another just to "keep busy." Rest assured that, after a while, it becomes easier to be alone and to tolerate being in the house by yourself. One of the indications of healing is when you can do this again.

Another aspect relates to one's aging process. As we are aware of our own aging, it is normal to be concerned about who will take care of us as we get older. We don't want to be overly dependent on our adult children. This issue particularly comes up when you are ill and most acutely aware of your "aloneness." The buddy-system is a good idea. As you make friends in a bereavement support group and bond, call each other during the week and socialize. Just be aware that this is a normal concern.

Q: *Do you think it helps to keep a journal?*

A: Anne Frank said, "paper is more patient and ... I don't intend to show this cardboard-covered notebook to anyone."

Often, when we record our feelings on paper, they make more sense. Some of us are able to cry and express our grief, while others are more private. Using *The Healing Power of Thought Workbook* in the second half of this book is a good place to explore, in quiet moments, feelings we are struggling with. Many people find relief and calmness after writing, just pouring out their hearts and then being able to walk away for awhile. Sometimes, putting thoughts and questions on paper allows you to open your heart in a way that hasn't been expressed out loud. Allow yourself to write, without judgment, whatever you're feeling. Journaling is a useful, healing tool.

Q: *Why are some people able to form a close relationship with another soon after their loss while others have such a problem with dating?*

A: Most people do want to connect again — some for friendship, others for companionship, and still others for love. Some people cannot tolerate being alone. Everyone, however, is different in their readiness and desires. Some may lack the opportunity. But, as a general rule, when we are frantic and needy, we make bad choices in our search to stop our pain.

As you begin to heal, you are not only more emotionally available to yourself, but you become available to others again. Also, the stage of your life is relevant to how you might go about searching for another relationship. Regardless of age, people often meet others in bereavement support groups because that common bond of grief offers a "comfort zone" with others in the same position. Sometimes these relationships begin with friendship and move on to love.

Q: *If you lose more than one person within six months or a year, can the grief overlap and how do you separate your feelings so that you can go through the process in the most beneficial way?*

A: When there are several losses in a brief time span, because the losses overlap the grieving may be confusing. It is not always clear who you are grieving for at any given time. In a way, it doesn't matter. The psyche when overwhelmed can shut down and that is not, necessarily, a bad thing.

We use our defenses to protect ourselves. We can't always separate-out our feelings. There are also different kinds of losses which may overlap, such as the loss of someone we love and the loss of status, home, job, or several relatives dying within a year. Regardless, the emphasis needs to be on healing *your* feelings. When loses overlap, wondering which stage of grief you are in may be less relevant, as the focus is on developing strategies to love life again. Healing slowly day by day, discussing the various losses with those you love ... crying, calling friends ... striving with humor to be yourself and acknowledging a very difficult time in your life can provide the best strategy.

Q: *How am I supposed to feel when I have something to share and my spouse is not there? There is no one next to me in bed to wake up with and the emptiness comes over me physically as well as emotionally.*

A: We experience loneliness on several levels. There is the loss of the physical presence of your spouse. You miss being hugged and touched. There is also the emotional bond of sharing, that desire to share thoughts and feelings with someone you are close to and feel emotionally connected to. Part of the sadness of grieving is recognizing that the one you most want to share with is gone.

Gradually you will be able to tolerate your own "aloneness" and will be able to reach out for new companionship and friendship.

Q: *After my husband passed away, I became very fearful of being ill and having no one to take care of me. How can I deal with that fear?*

A: It is scary and anxiety-provoking because this fear reminds you that you are now alone and potentially dependent on others. Besides missing the support of your spouse, you may question your ability to take adequate care of yourself. Often, there is resistance to being dependent on friends and family. When you are in need of support, love, caring and attention, it is a painful reminder of the fragility of life and it is important that you work through those feelings and accept help.

Moving Toward Healing

How will you know when you have begun healing?

By being emotionally available to yourself.

By having the recognition of healing *moments* within the day.

By being present and "in the moment."

By acknowledging breathing and breath.

By remembering that life is worth living and loving.

By having the ability to maintain a positive attitude.

By having the ability to be patient with yourself.

By giving yourself permission to feel whatever you feel.

By allowing for moments of joy, as well as sadness.

By giving yourself permission to be alive in the face of death.

By eventually experiencing enjoyment and laughter.

By welcoming the return of energy and love of life.

Healing allows you to be whole again. You will do it slowly and with consciousness. It's not as if suddenly you will wake up one day and you are whole. Part of the major task of grieving is to find out who you are, now that you are alone. You might have to take over functions that your spouse provided; the division of labor is different now. The rebalancing might include such everyday tasks as pumping gas or cooking simple meals, which you never did before.

Healing is a lot about attitude and determination, the will and the ability to take on the work of healing. It is resisting the desire to lie down and die on days that are difficult. It is deciding that you want to survive, and to go beyond survival and enjoy life again. If you are too overwhelmed or sad or non-functional, it would be wise to seek counseling, and possibly consider medications from your doctor for a boost of mood. Such a decision implies emotional health rather than illness; a recognition that you are in trouble and want help.

Healing allows for, and provides permission for, mood changes ... allows you to be where you are emotionally. Sometimes you push yourself, and sometimes you go with the flow of a mood. For example, if you are an extrovert, you allow for sometimes being an introvert. The psyche wants to seek balance when it's out of kilter.

Healing recognizes that others want to help, or to just stand by. Sometimes, there is little else the person can do but stand by and listen, and that is a great deal.

Healing includes: the role of love, returning to wholeness, listening to your own innate wisdom, a healing attitude, and the realization that healing is our natural state.

The most common feeling during these first four months of mourning is simply, shock.

Understanding Shock

Shock is an alarm response to a sudden, violent or upsetting disturbance. Whether the loss is sudden or expected, the element of shock is still present. It is an alarm state that protects you from the flood of emotions with which you may be unable to cope. Whether experienced as anxiety, insomnia and/or numbness, it actually helps the mourner get through this initial time period.

Laura's late husband, Paul, died suddenly. "It was totally unexpected," says Laura. "The memorial service wasn't held until ten days later and in some ways this delay was good because it gave everyone a chance to gather and collect their thoughts. Her late husband's large family includes a sister and brother, and a large extended family of many cousins, who gave a great deal of family support. "My sisters were also incredible; within hours of Richard's passing my sisters and their husbands arrived from their homes in northern California to be with me. One of my sisters stayed for 12 days. While here, they helped to arrange everything, they were wonderful." A dear friend living in Australia got on a plane and stayed an additional two weeks, helping Laura pick up the pieces and run the family business. "I was understandably a total wreck.

"During those first 10 days, there were probably 25 people in her home at any given time. The dining table was groaning with food, and at times it was overwhelming. But I gave myself complete permission to just disappear and be alone in another room. I also told my kids, two boys 14 and 20-years-old, that when they needed to take a break from our houseful of people, it was okay to disappear into their bedrooms."

SHOCK CAN BE felt even when death is expected due to illness. We think we're prepared, yet ...

Ruthe's husband died at 8:30AM on October 28, 2003. Her immediate reaction to his death was relief, "because he had been suffering from the last stages of Parkinson's Disease, unable to move his arms or legs or able to talk. He would look at me and I could only guess at what he might be thinking, or if he was thinking at all.

"I thought I was prepared to lose him since everything inside me told me that his life had no quality and that he would not choose to live if in fact, he had a choice. I was so wrong. Intellectually I was prepared but emotionally the roller coaster began. The relief was over so quickly I cannot, at this point almost eighteen months later, recall the feeling at all, just the emptiness that I felt knowing that he was really gone and never coming back." Ruthe felt that her life was over after almost fifty eight years of a good marriage with an intelligent, witty, loving and loyal man.

She had never lived alone. "I came from my mother's house to our life together and we were rarely apart. We worked together in our business, socialized together with our friends and spent time together in our retirement. We each had friends but in truth, we were each other's best friend.

"My cousin prodded me to go to a bereavement support group after Gene died. He said 'you have been mourning his loss a long time, you need to go.' He even talked to the facilitating therapist to help arrange a ride for me so that I would have no excuse to stay home. I went and found that it was somewhat comforting to be in the company of others who were experiencing some of the same emotions I felt, however, I felt different than the others; I thought I must be crazy because of the myriad of emotions I was feeling."

Ruthe was surprised to find herself in denial over her husband's passing. As decisions to be made came up, she would think "I have to talk to Gene about that." It was a painful reminder that he was truly gone. "I would suddenly get a terrible feeling of dread and then I would remember that he was gone and I would never see him again. It happened over and over again."

The bereavement support group helped her to realize that the "craziness" she was feeling was all part of the grief process. However, at that point Ruthe was hospitalized with an Electrolyte imbalance and unable to attend her bereavement support group. Once home, she was hesitant to return. Once again her cousin urged her on. "As soon as I came home from the hospital, my cousin was there urging, no, insisting that I go back to the support group." Ruthe did and "within two meetings I knew I still needed this group, not only for the grief support, but the companionship. We started meeting before group for dinner and that helped solidify our friendships.

"Our discussions were so open and so honest about all of our fears and our hopes, we likened it to feeling like a family and we clung together like survivors from a sinking ship. We looked forward to our meetings and in between some of our wonderful members planned outings or invited us to parties in their homes."

Ruthe had not felt capable at that point of socializing outside of her immediate family and "my support group opened my world and let sunshine into my life. Slowly, I found myself smiling more and even laughing out loud, something I hadn't done for months. I discovered that most of the crazy feelings I had were shared by others in the group. We were feeling overwhelmed with details and paperwork, procrastinating when most of us had been efficient and prompt before grief struck us.

"We shared our feelings of dread before visiting the cemetery for the first time after the funeral and the anxiety of choosing a proper (and perfect) marker for our loved one's resting place. No subject was off limits. Soon members were beginning to have serious relationships, some within the group and some outside. All were discussed and encouraged by the rest of us who were not so fortunate as to have found companionship and love. It has been very interesting to watch the grieving process continue even as new relationships were formed.

"It has now been almost seventeen months since my dear husband's death. I am still lonely and miss the love we shared but I know now that I must go on and find purpose in my life. After many years of care giving, I must even re-discover and re-invent myself."

Ruthe shares this moving tribute to Gene:

He is gone, his footsteps removed from my sight but not my memory
His voice, now silent but still in my head reminding me of his kindness and wisdom
His touch, so gentle and loving, now missing from my life
His humor, still vivid in mind but lost to my soul
His love, with me always but nothing I can touch, feel or smell

His sense of fairness, now lost to the world but remembered by all who loved him

His grace, I can see him moving, walking, touching the things he loved but they are lonely now too

His guidance, it is remembered but cannot be heard, it kept my feet on the right path

His wonderful smile and laugh, etched in my memory like a fine Rembrandt or Durer

He is missing from my life but he left his footprints in my heart and will be with me forever."

"It has been said that 'what doesn't kill you, makes you stronger' and I firmly believe that is true. I have watched the people in my group deal with their losses and struggle with loneliness, fear of the future and just about every emotion you can experience. They have all grown stronger, as I have, and though they still have ups and downs most are coping much better because of the support offered by this wonderful group," addsRuthe.

What are the symptoms of shock? You may experience shock as anxiety, insomnia, or even numbness. In early shock, people are frequently overwhelmed. You may cry at the drop of a hat, have trouble sleeping, eating and relaxing. You have difficulties concentrating. You may be able to function fine at work, but when you get home, you can't read the newspaper or remember what you are reading. It is difficult to focus. You may suffer a loss of self-esteem.

You may feel as if you are on "automatic pilot," or "numb." It is common to misplace keys; lose things and forget appointments. All of this is normal. You may feel overwhelmed with paperwork. "Processing" all of your feelings might be impossible. Later, when time has passed, more feelings return and shock may fold into depression as reality comes into focus. But for now, this early shock offers protection from feelings that would be unmanageable at this point in your mourning. Shock is a defense of the ego, and as such, designed to protect you. Healing can be compared to a surgical wound, raw at first; it then begins to heal from the inside out, layer by layer. And, even when it is healed, the wound can still be tender to the touch when bumped; healing is raw and it takes time.

However, while shock helps you get through the initial period following loss, there is also a much more dangerous side to shock to be aware of, one which can affect your physical health.

"A personal trauma like losing a loved one can literally break your heart," suggests new research reported by, *The Week*, February 25, 2005, "Health & Science." According to the story, "Doctors at Baltimore's Johns Hopkins University have identified a condition— nicknamed "broken heart syndrome"—that can be brought on by sudden emotional stress, caused by a death in the family, an armed robbery, or even a surprise party. These types of traumas can lead to heart failure in some people, especially women. During a one year period, 18 women and one man were hospitalized in Baltimore with cardiac failure after such shocks," the researchers report in the *New England Journal of Medicine*.

Symptoms of broken heart syndrome mimic those of a heart attack, but it is not the same thing. A heart attack occurs when a blood clot in a coronary artery cuts off circulation to the heart muscle. But broken heart syndrome occurs when a blast of adrenaline stuns the heart muscle, leaving it temporarily unable to contract. Patients diagnosed with the condition were all previously healthy, with no history of heart disease. The findings, researcher Dr. Ilan S. Wittstein tells *The New York Times,* lend support to the folk wisdom that sorrow or fright can be fatal. "It's important for people to know that this is something that emotional stress truly can do," he said.

Helpful Do's and Don'ts

Helpful Do's and Don'ts for the Bereaved

Do call a friend when you are blue.

Do water the flowers and take time to smell them; work in the garden, pull out weeds.

Do something positive for yourself every day.

Do get enough sleep.

Do exercise daily.

Do remember to take time to eat.

Do think positive thoughts every day.

Do spend time with family and friends.

Do get as much support as you can.

Do open the mail.

Do treasure your loved ones.

Do resist the temptation to run away from your pain by keeping yourself *frantically* busy every waking moment.

Do journal in a notebook about your feelings.

Do see a therapist if you feel constantly overwhelmed.

Do allow people to help you.

Do be patient with yourself.

Do take your own car to an event, so you can leave when you want to.

Do be grateful for what you have.

Do allow enough time for healing.

Do watch funny movies.

Do listen to quiet music.

Do create positive affirmations about yourself.

Do pursue a satisfying creative outlet.

Do stay focused on specifics to help you get through the day.

Don't stay in bed the entire day.

Don't do things you don't want to do if you feel pushed into them by well meaning friends.

Don't stay too isolated.

Don't turn invitations away.

Don't overindulge in alcohol or sweets.

Don't be disappointed in yourself, grief takes more energy than you would ever have imagined.

Don't throw out or give away the clothes until you are ready.

Don't write thank you notes until you feel up to it.

Don't, if possible, make any major lifestyle changes or decisions … for now.

Helpful Do's and Don'ts for Friends and Family of the Bereaved

The bereaved often feel upset by the things people say to them. Of course, they often feel that nothing is a comfort and anything that is said is offensive. If we are feeling terribly wounded, words don't comfort, while comforting hugs or an arm around your shoulder feel much better. Statements and questions such as, "How are you doing?" Or, "Are you doing better?" or "It's hard for me, it must be terrible for you," *do not* feel good when we are in the shock of mourning.

Don't say you understand when you don't understand how someone else feels. Say, "I'm sorry for your loss and your pain" instead of "I understand how you feel."

Don't patronize the bereaved.

Don't forget to call several weeks after the funeral.

Don't walk away from friends because they have lost their spouse.

Please turn to page 224
for the Workbook section on this Time Sequence.

3.

Time Sequences of Healing Grief
Months Five through Eight
Denial

THE MENTAL FOG THAT *had sheltered me emotionally during those first four months is slowly, and painfully, beginning to clear. Coincidently, this occurs just as the world around me appears to need me to get out and on with my life. And so, I'm finding that this is an important time in my mourning because with my newfound awareness comes the need to take a stand, to "own" my grieving process. Sounds like I'm getting stronger? Yes, in some ways, but the reality is that sadness, crying and feeling lost are still very much a part of my day-to-day world.*

Two weeks shy of the fifth-month anniversary of my husband's death, I can say, without the slightest hesitation or hint of exaggeration that grieving sucks. Ugly word? Yes. Ugly feeling? Absolutely! Grieving is neither gentle nor quiet; it is bottomless loneliness, anger and depression, until finally, a year or two down the road, I will be at peace with my loss -- or so the experts say.

But for now, there's no way around my grief; I can't hide from it (for long anyway) or run away from it -- it follows me wherever I go, no matter how fast I'm travelin'. I'm reminded, painfully once again, that losing a spouse is different from any other loss.

When my husband died after a prolonged illness, I thought I was prepared for his death. And I was - intellectually. What I now know is that we can prepare our intellect, but when death happens, emotionally, it still feels as if you are slamming into a brick wall. The rhythms of life continue around me unaltered, but I feel as if the universe is out of kilter, even on my best days.

Feeling so raw, what did I do to try to take care of myself at a time when I felt incapable of dealing with anything? Thankfully support was available in a variety of forms. All it took was my willingness to take life baby step-by baby-step and work hard to keep an open heart and mind. The following steps I found to be helpful.

Bereavement Support Group

Profound grief was, for me, deeply isolating, because although family and friends wanted to help, it was impossible for them to relate to what I was going through. Instead, I joined a bereavement support group run by professional counselors, which made the experience more manageable. It gave the process structure and me a place where each week, no matter what else was going on in my life, my grieving was encouraged. I joined a support group -- even though the thought of being with strangers was, at that time, the last thing I felt capable of doing.

No matter what other challenges I was dealing with, this was a place for me to fully know my sorrow. By its very structure, a bereavement group offers a sort of marker, one that allows you to appreciate your own ups and downs, as well as your progress. Sure, you'll cry in front of people you don't know, but they'll cry as well. And eventually, you'll cry less and laugh more as you cherish the emotional safety this group provides. You'll also feel good about helping other group members, which in turn helps you to begin to feel powerful and whole again.

You might feel afraid that it's like going to therapy, something that might be especially scary when you're so vulnerable. Be assured that while a licensed bereavement therapist moderates the group, this is a "support" process group that deals with the here and now, it is not a therapy group that delves into your childhood in order to resolve old issues.

At this point in my mourning, these have been my most important discoveries:

Honor YOURSELF

Recognize who among family, friends, neighbors, and co-workers are emotionally safe right now and base your expectations on that information. Trust your ability to sense with whom you can be vulnerable, and with whom you cannot. My saddest moments are when something wonderful happens and my husband isn't there to celebrate or congratulate. By the same token, I've also lost the one person I could always go to when I needed a break from life's everyday problems. He wasn't there so much to fix things, but to provide a place to rest when I needed it. It's not the same, or quite as good, but I turn to others for that, for now.

Honor yourself and your need to put yourself first ... for now. This is hard if your spouse passed away from a prolonged illness and you were, as I was, his caregiver. I'm just beginning to realize how, over the challenging care-giving years, I'd lost the ability to be spontaneous—too many doctors, dialysis, pills, procedures to be aware of, not to mention my husband's inability to be left alone for *more than an hour at a time, and even then, I was never far. Doctor appointments, medical treatments, medications, the to-do's were many, so much so that taking care of my own needs quickly fell to the bottom of the list. Our lives revolved around my husband's illness. Now is your time to re-learn the art of spontaneity, to have adventures and fun, and to take care of yourself.*

Be open with your adult children about your grief and the process you're going through. Just please remind them that it's not their job to take care of your grief or to make your grief disappear. First of all, no one can make your grief disappear; it is a process you will work through. They can support your effort; they just can't do it for you. Second, by example, you will encourage them to process their own grief in an honest, open way, allowing all of you to remain emotionally open to each other.

Take care of your inner child. No matter what your current chronological age, you have a lonely, scared child inside. Honor his or her need to feel safe. Not sure what that means? Sit comfortably in a quiet place, close your eyes gently and let your mind wander. Picture yourself at whatever age comes to you. Three, seven, twelve ... that's your inner child. Gently place that child on your lap and enfold that child in your arms. In your head, ask that very special person what he or she needs from you, the adult, in order to feel safe again. Trust me, he or she will let you know, all you need do is to pay attention, to listen.

Slow down. Meditate, nap, sit in the garden, smell the roses. The exact opposite of keeping yourself busy, busy, busy. Sure, busy might keep you from having time to think, but you also won't heal.

Exercise. God/Mother Nature/The Universe blessed us with endorphins. Our body's own feel-good high; it's natural and it's free. Allow this brain chemical to neutralize stress hormones to help you feel better. All your endorphins need is a little stimulation (experience tells me that it takes only a half hour of brisk walking to kick into gear.) Exercise need not be brutal, just regular.

Better living through chemistry. Your doctor may recommend antidepressant medication to help you cope during this difficult time. Be aware that this medication can take up to three weeks of daily dosage to produce results, and understand that an antidepressant medication is not the same as a tranquilizer. A tranquilizer will take the edge off your pain minutes after it is taken, but only give you relief for a period of hours. It can also make you feel sedated, which might be a very unpleasant feeling when your entire life feels as if it's out of control. An antidepressant, once it has built up in your system over a period of weeks, will simply make the world feel more manageable; you, however, will not feel sedated.

Timetables. Honor your own timetable for sorting out your spouse's personal things, for changing the message on the answering machine, and taking care of the other pending tasks. The added tragedy of loss is that many of us are also left to cope with the mechanics of a business and must contend with all of this at a time when we feel unable to cope with anything. Look to family, professionals, and trusted friends -- don't be afraid to ask for help.

Yesterday, Today and Tomorrow

Live in the moment, for that's all we have any control over. The past is gone and the future holds no guarantees. Moment-to-moment, celebrate life, or rage at the forces, but stay present. For me, taking care of "the now" included honoring those close friends of my husband's who were also struggling with this loss. I wrapped personal objects of my husband's, a treasured fountain pen, a tie, little objects from his desk at the office and sent them with a note letting each person know how special their friendship had been to my husband. It gave me a way to gracefully put closure to relationships that I knew would not survive his death because they had been his. I was uncomfortable allowing these special people to just drift without closure.

Five months in, that's all I know for now—but I'll keep learning, making mistakes, growing stronger, feeling sad when I least expect it, and living. Oh, and yes, reminding myself to breathe now and then as I begin to feel strong enough to once again reach for my joy.

Common Questions

When will the pain lessen?

When will I have a life again?

What will my life look like?

What should I do on the days I want to do nothing?

How can I think about a future, when I'm not even sure about the "Now?"

My future was going to be with him; how can I know how to develop a life for myself, when I don't know what my "self" is?

How do I forgive myself the guilt of "what I should have done, might have done or could have done" at the end of his life?

I know it's important to try to stay in the Now, but what do I do when my mind wanders and I go into future or past mode?

What helps me stay in the Now? How do people do that?

When I feel out of control, what's a good way to feel in control again?

I've always had some anxiety; now it's even worse. Do you have suggestions as to how to work with that?

I'm not ready for dating. How do people move to that readiness? I'm frightened of "stepping out there," and I'm not ready to take risks.

THE PAIN LESSENS AS healing takes place. Healing takes place slowly and at a different rate for different people. Think of it as a surgical scar; you heal from the inside out, layer by layer. Yet, even when it finally heals, it may still be sensitive.

How do you cope with the word "never?" *He's never coming back* is a statement that you suffer through yet don't want to hear. Inside your heart, you may know that it's true, but you don't want to *hear* that reality. In their mistaken attempt to offer comfort, people often say to the bereaved, "They are in a better place"... and you want to scream, "But what about me?" At this point, you are searching for some kind of inner peace. It is as if you are walking around in the world in a suit that feels constantly too small. One size does not fit everyone, it was never meant to.

Will I ever feel whole again or will I forever feel tarnished? Do you hate the words "widow or widower" because it makes you feel odd, different, a changed status that you did not want or ask for?

Feeling Out Of Control

"In my case," says Laura, "Richard died so suddenly; it changed *everything* and *everyone* in my life. Prior to his death I was teaching part time, I was about to go back to school to get my Master's Degree in psychology. I'd wanted to do this for a long time and had talked about it for a long time, and finally, at this point in our lives, Richard was all for it." Laura was all set up, even registered to return to school at the end of the summer. Richard owned a lumber business that was finally doing well and he was looking forward to selling it.

The plan was for Laura to take over as breadwinner once she had a practice going and Richard thought that was great. When he died, Laura had to abandon all her plans and take care of the family business. Two days after his death she was writing out payroll checks. "I had to start overseeing the business and it was overwhelming, especially as I had no real ability or affinity for it and suddenly I just had to do it." Thankfully Laura had several loyal employees who were very helpful, but ultimately, she was responsible for the business, their home and their children. "Richard used to do everything and suddenly this was all my baby and there was just so much on my plate. I also felt that I couldn't fall apart because I had children to care for."

At that time, Laura was the Mayor of her city, served on the school board where she once taught, and had other involvements that she couldn't abandon. She felt that her distractions had a positive effect. "People told me I was too busy and that I should pull back, but what was I going to do ... just go home and feel bad? I really am convinced that you can mourn and do a whole lot of other things at the same time. Being busy was in many ways a blessing for me.

"What was probably most difficult was confronting the loss of the family unit and the reality that my sons had lost their father."

One of the main issues during these months is control, since you are still getting past the feeling of helplessness. For example, in the past you could not prevent your spouse from dying and thus you are feeling out of control in your present life. New tasks and roles have been thrust upon you, and often you feel inadequate in these new roles. You are understandably frustrated, which can, in turn, lead to anger. The new anger merges with the old anger at losing your spouse. The "Why did they have to die?" anger is fused with the "Why did this happen to me?" anger.

You are now coming out of your shock, and as you do, you begin to feel things with a greater intensity. This leads to the common fear of going backward in your grieving, feeling as badly, or even worse than you had when your spouse first died. These fears are normal and you are not "slipping backwards" or losing control completely. The reality is that you have forgotten the intensity of the pain you felt at the beginning of your mourning, the pain that caused you to turn on "automatic pilot" or freeze your emotions in order to just get through the day. When shock begins to wear off and reality sets in, feelings return, so emotions are felt more intensely.

What should you do on the days when you want to do nothing? Some days it is hard to get out of bed, you just want to pull the covers up and hide from the world. On other days, the sun beckons. For the days that nothing is on the agenda, the lack of structure may be very difficult and can add to your depression. Having something to do each day is beneficial because it gives you something to look forward to. A change of scenery can help, too: go into the garden and snip the roses, appreciate their beauty, feed them so they can grow and thrive. A change of scene can be as close as your own backyard.

It is important on days when you want to do nothing to get up, get dressed, walk, call a friend, get out of the house, go to a mall, see a movie, or call someone who loves you. Let them know how good it feels just to hear their voice, that you just need to connect, but aren't looking for rah-rah encouragement. A good friend understands this, especially if they have been there themselves.

Group Support

Joining a bereavement support group provides a roadmap for healing. It is a positive step, even if, at first, you don't feel capable of attending. Within a group, people talk and people listen, giving you the opportunity to take what you can use and leave the rest behind. It is important to share your feelings in order to learn that you are not alone and crazy. Feeling crazy in bereavement doesn't mean you are; it means your world is upside down and backwards and nothing makes sense. There is tremendous validation in the company of others who have also lost a partner or mate. Another advantage of attending a bereavement support group is that members often reflect later on something that they heard in group and find it helpful.

"After almost 54 years of marriage," explains Hal, "my beloved and beautiful soul mate, my wife, passed away suddenly in her sleep at 3:20 a.m. I was totally unprepared as she had no chronic illness." Hal says he became a complete basket case, languishing in bed for two weeks, drugged and barely coherent. If it hadn't been for his children's love, he says he would have opted to leave the planet. Instead, he took his children's advice and agreed to see a therapist they said could help him. "They were right."

Hal's therapist repeatedly suggested he join a bereavement support group, and his answer always was, "No Way." Finally, out of respect for her, he reluctantly promised to attend at least three meetings. "As I told the group at my first meeting, I was 'dragged in kicking and screaming.' But to coin a well worn phrase 'the rest is history.'

"I now attribute a great deal of my ability to cope with the grieving process to attending this group these last several months. The obvious experience of sharing with those who are in the same boat with you is healing in itself, not to mention the lasting friendships that are developed." Hal still takes an antidepressant medication once a day, still sees his therapist twice a week, and is certain the bereavement support group has and is playing a major role in his being able to continue living, "Not as I knew it but as I must now understand it."

His grief still manifests itself when he is alone and memories of his past life come flooding back. "I still ride a rollercoaster of emotions throughout the week but when Thursday comes and I attend my group a tiny bit of healing occurs. And that's good."

Hal attributes the helpfulness of the group to an atmosphere of understanding, because members are all going through a similar experience. "And the primary benefit of a group is that you become aware that many feelings you thought were only your own, are truly those of almost everyone else's in the group. We had so much commonality that I think 'commonality' would be the key word."

However, not all bereavement support groups are right for everyone. Listen to your inner voice. If a group doesn't help you, it would be wise to look for another. That's what Laura decided to do.

After joining an online support group, she soon realized that the focus was and continued to be only on feelings that occur immediately after a loss. But Laura wanted to move beyond that first phase, to learn how to function, and how to reach a better place emotionally. After four or five months she realized the group didn't seem to be about that at all.

The online support group helped initially because through it, Laura came to understand that she wasn't 'losing it,' that other people were experiencing the same feelings as she was. "What I found discouraging was that some people seemed to have just latched on to this as their identity. They'd been checking in with the group for as long as two and three years and I thought, Oh gosh, I don't want to stay here."

Anxiety

There may be a great deal of anxiety at this time; not only are you feeling out of control, which causes anxiety, but you are often feeling conflicting emotions. One moment everything seems dismal or dark, then for a few moments there seems to be some hope or peace. Then, just as suddenly, these disappear and fear takes over again. You want a magic 'fix' to make you feel complete again. So much so that questions such as "When will the emptiness go away? When will I feel good again?" are frequent and persistent, and you want to know if these are normal, common concerns. You want and need validation for your feelings and thoughts.

Reframing

A very useful technique at this point is "reframing." When we change the way in which we think about things, we change our feelings about it; reframing means changing your perception of something, such as an event, by understanding it in another way.

Reframing your feelings about your loss will help you view it with less pain, because seeing things in a variety of ways builds understanding. No, this technique cannot change the situation, but the meaning is changed. For example, death is a life event that has different meanings in different cultures, and individuals deal with it in vastly different ways. Some are forever grieving the loss, whereas others are joyous at the now eternal presence of the person's spirit. In other words, different people attach very different meanings and interpretations to the concept of death.

Reframing means taking an experience that seems negative, and exploring how the same experience could be positive in another context. Each of us perceives the world as it filters through our frames of perception. Thus, each of us finds unique meaning in our world.

Reframing, then, expands our perceptions by providing a new lens through which to view life. What may be a disastrous problem for one person is a challenging growth opportunity for another. Victor E. Frankl, Ph.D., author of *Man's Search for Meaning* and a Nazi Concentration Camp survivor recounted that although most of his fellow inmates lost hope and subsequently died; he kept hope and planned for the lectures he would give after his release. In his own mind, he turned a potentially hopeless situation into a source of rich experiences that he could later use to help others overcome hopeless situations. Fortunately, we do not have to be in such dire circumstances for reframing to be useful. Every moment of every day, there is opportunity to see things in another way. To see through another frame of perception can give us hope and a better perspective of ourselves and others.

There are no correct frames of perceptions. There are only useful frames and not so useful frames, depending on the situation. However, a useful reframe is to understand that all perceptions are useful in some context.

Firsts

During this time, many "firsts" come up. First birthday, anniversary, and holidays occur and you are understandably apprehensive. You anticipate each occurrence with dread, wondering if you can get "through" the date. Be somewhat assured that anticipation is frequently worse than the actual event and can be softened by recalling past experiences when that was true.

At this point, you might attempt to look into your future to try to determine what you want to do with the rest of your life. Or you might still be facing life one day at a time, or one week or month at a time. Even if you feel able to look down the road a bit, don't be surprised to find confusion and perhaps guilt. The guilt is that if you start a "new" life via dating, are you then disloyal to your deceased spouse. You worry about what others will say, especially your children. You sometimes feel ambivalent about wanting to enjoy life again, and "what will the deceased spouse think?"

Dating

Your readiness for dating should always be on your own timetable, and not when friends and family think that "it's time to get over your mourning and get on with your life." You may still feel uncomfortable about dating, not only because of guilt, but because it's something you have not done for twenty, thirty, or forty years. Now, the belief system of your distant teenage past must be reconciled with the adult beliefs you hold today. Behaving as you did many years ago does not work or feel right for you anymore.

You don't know what is expected of the single adult of the 2006's, so you will be going through adolescence again, in the true sense of the word, because adolescence is a time to try out new things. It is time to question what you want to do for the rest of your life, a time to find one's self. All of this is part of the process as you weather the pain of death, emerge from the cocoon of shock and denial, and move toward integration, adjustment and transition.

Control

Gaining control over your life is one issue, while facing a permanent reality of losing your spouse is another, both often coupled with the fear of, "Will this be the rest of my life? How do I define myself as separate from him or her? Where we used to overlap, now I am alone and faced with decisions about which I used to consult with him or her."

The sense of aloneness and possibly facing future illness as a person "alone" can feel terrifying. You want to be independent *and* you want to be cared for, yet you don't want to lean on your adult children too much. As in your teen age years, you want to be both dependent and independent. "Are my adult kids calling too much? Or, Do they not call enough? If I am sick and alone, how will I manage?"

The future represents an unknown, and thinking about a future alone can create anxiety. As a self-reliant person, you may begin to recognize how much you value the support of your family yet not want to lean too heavily on your grown children, who are busy with their own lives. At the same time, you are appreciative of their attention. You want to be with them and with other family members, but you don't want to overstep boundaries. Sometimes your grown children may include you, for example, in their travel plans, and that feels good; but your feelings of pride, wanting to pay your own way, and remain independent are understandable.

The decision-making process is much harder if you are used to discussing concerns with your partner, such as a widow, who was in business with her husband, misses having his opinions and feedback, if he was the only one she felt comfortable sharing with. You may feel overwhelmed with doing your share and "their" share and making decisions on your own, particularly if your spouse took care of the monetary aspects of your life. For example, you may know how to use the checkbook, but for the most part were not involved in the investments. Some people are comfortable and familiar dealing with those aspects, and others are not. Some are able to seek out professionals to advise them, while others may turn to their grown children. Still others may be wary of stepping into a world that looks foreign to them.

If you are overcome with grief and have to make monetary decisions, it is wise to wait if you can, however, regardless of the time span, seek counsel and weigh the advice you hear. If you are not clear, question. If you don't understand, ask again. Don't make financial decisions at a time when you are overcome with stress, don't understand, or are too bewildered to think clearly. The early grief period is not the time to tackle areas where you are inexperienced. Go slowly. Gain confidence and knowledge gradually and make sure that grief does not interfere with appropriate decision making.

Holidays can bring additional anxieties and a host of mixed feelings. When other families are celebrating together, or attending church or synagogue, you might sense your own aloneness, even if you are with your family members. Nonetheless, the surrounding family love can be a comfort and reliable foundation for the bereaved.

Forgiveness
How do you forgive yourself the guilt of "What I should have done," or, "What I might have done" or, "What I could have done at the end of his life?" It is normal to rehash actions that were taken. Once again, in retrospect, many widows and widowers even imagine that if certain alternatives had been taken, their spouse might still be alive.

Be aware that this is a way of holding on. It is important to learn to let go, not of the person, but of your feelings of inner torment. To quote Albert Ellis, Ph.D., "Don't *should* on yourself." Another common thought is, "If only I hadn't left the room at that moment, he/she would still be alive because I could have called 911 sooner." Or, "If only I hadn't stopped at the market on my way home from work, he/she would not have had the heart attack." There are dozens of scenarios and a great need for forgiveness: self-forgiveness for being a less than perfect person; forgiveness toward others who have wronged us; forgiveness to the physician who may have made a mistake. Recognize that in your moment of medical decision, *you made the best decision you could with the facts at hand.* Additional facts are always known later. Try not to look back over your shoulder. Self-forgiveness is so important, and another step in the direction of healing.

Forgive your spouse for leaving you, and recognize that they didn't intend to "leave you." They had to. They had to because they were too sick to recover or circumstances were such that their bodies didn't enable them to live anymore.

Something magnificent happens when you forgive yourself. You reach a new level of freedom and are, to a degree, freed from inner turmoil and anguish. This happens slowly and is not a sudden revelation. When you are freed of some pain you might experience it as an expanded emotional space in which to care for yourself. But you have to be willing to let go of some pain to enable yourself to move forward. Healing has many aspects. Something wonderful emerges when you can free yourself of self judgment and criticism. You may be your own worst critic; or, chances are someone was critical of you if this is a continuing theme for yourself. To forgive yourself is a wonderful step forward.

When we are emotionally "stuck," we are glued to our old belief system. When we can reframe, i.e., change the meaning of our behavior, we change the way we feel about it. The behavior we thought was ours shifts to have another meaning. It softens. Often, we are so locked into our belief system of the past that our regrets are lived out in the present.

While mourning, you may fear being "stuck" in one of the stages and not know how to move forward. Are you stuck in denial? In anger? Is your "stuck-ness" functional for you? Does it exist because movement represents healing and you are not ready to heal your loss? Do you have to participate willingly in your own healing, and if you choose to do so, what emerges? Perhaps unconsciously, you want to wallow in pain and regrets longer than is useful because you are afraid to move forward, and know no other way. The path of pain is familiar; forgiveness and the willingness to move on are not. Moving on requires courage at a time when you feel depleted, yet it is wholesome, rewarding and necessary. It is important to wholeheartedly participate in your own healing by recognizing that we have made a conscious choice to do so. "Re-framing" allows you to develop a larger life vision, one that works toward creating a well-balanced life.

Creating a Well-Balanced Life

Support groups make a major contribution in the life of a person dealing with grief. Feedback from the other participants and validation from the facilitator are so vital. Developing the whole person is a combination of intellectual, psychological and emotional facets. Joining a self-help group; psychotherapy; taking classes at a local college; participating in a study group; learning meditation; reading non-fiction all contribute to one's personal growth. Enjoyment of the learning process will help you move out of grief and back into life. Then the evolving self moves to the threshold of the next step, spirituality.

Spirituality involves openness to something that is larger than oneself. This heightened state of consciousness may be achieved through meditation, nature or prayer. While pondering the meaning of life, for instance, you may also become interested in understanding the nature of the universe. Spirituality is an indefinable experience and may occur when we see the ocean, view a sunset, or when we connect with another human being. It is a sense of renewal that comes from connecting within ourselves and to a higher power. There is a positive correlation between spirituality and recovery.

Participating in sports or hobbies on a regular basis will enhance your sense of well-being, providing a respite from everyday activities and a chance to renew yourself without pressure. The activities may be sedentary and indoors or physical and outdoors. Golf, photography, collecting, hiking, walking, sailing and biking all fall into this category. The activity would have to be regularly enjoyed, but not necessarily daily or weekly. Movies, theatre and museum visits can add cultural exposure and enhance your sense of well-being.

How you eat, exercise and take care of your body influences the mind/body connection in a positive way. Food is the fuel that runs the machine that creates the life we want. Being mindful of fast foods with high fat content and participating in a regular fitness program are important components of a balanced life. There is abundant evidence indicating the positive effects of diet and exercise on emotional and physical well-being.

Often, a positive sign of healing is evident in a person's ability to give back to the community. At first you are understandably very involved with your own reactions and have trouble imagining beyond that. As time moves on, you are able to resume volunteer work again or take an interest in community involvement that you could not experience in the beginning. Such involvement is often correlated with happiness and even with physical health. People who participate in some form of community involvement, such as volunteering with non-profit groups or nursing homes or hospitals, live happier, more rewarding lives with fewer illnesses.

Widows and widowers who are still involved in their work world seem to sometimes have an easier adjustment because they have a focal point during the day. Having a focus outside of the home often prevents dwelling on loss. Career satisfaction plays an important part in one's overall feeling about oneself. We identify with our work and our profession. When we enjoy what we do for a living, and derive satisfaction from doing a job well, we feel better about ourselves. Fulfillment with work can affect our entire life.

Your family and friends are major contributors to your sense of fulfillment and happiness. Participating in daily family life, family conversations and recreational pursuits all help to create a sense of social well-being.

Keeping your financial house in order is extremely important for a sense of well-being. These include planning your finances carefully; keeping a budget; allocating for savings and investments; and planning for retirement. Having a living trust; a will; a living will; and planning for your own eventual death contribute to feeling in charge of your life and accepting responsibility for it. Although we recognize that these are important tasks to take care of, you can only do this at a time when sufficient grieving has taken place or you may feel overwhelmed. Seek the counsel of professional financial advisers when you are ready.

The Future

"My future was going to be with him. How can I know how to develop a life for myself when I don't know what my 'self' is?" The excitement of self discovery is a possibility for the future. Some may choose to stay "stuck," not progress or even go backwards, but the healthy individual eventually will get excited about possibilities as yet unexplored. You have more resilience than you know! Your inner psyche *wants* joy again, but at this point, does not know how to get there.

When there is inner trust once again, your real self will step forward to take on new and unexplored territories. Refuse to accept anything less than happiness in your life. Get there by being involved, by loving, by exploring new and old things that provide you with satisfaction for living.

Staying In the *Now*

"I like staying in the *now*, but what do I do when my mind wanders and I go into the past or future?" While this sounds like the buttons on a tape recorder, staying in the present means being just in this moment. It also means emptying the mind of the busy chatter, or acknowledging the chatter, not attaching to it, or expanding it. Let thoughts come and go at will, acknowledge them, and *breathe through it*. Staying in the *now* builds self-forgiveness and allows you to take mental breaks from thinking constantly about your loss. If you see a funny movie and you laugh, that's wonderful. There is an important connection between improving, moving forward and staying in the *now*.

Making a deliberate effort to stay in the *now* will help to get you through the difficult moments that continue to present themselves. In early bereavement, just getting through the *now* is enough. At that point, trying to take on the future would lead to feeling overwhelmed because the future still looks like a muddy page.

"Will I have a life again?" Living "life" requires energy, purpose, goals and a future. Early in bereavement, people can't see or feel a future. It all looks dark and dreary. As you heal, you will move forward into the light, the light that makes the darkness less scary. If you are in a pitch black cave and cannot see anything you are likely to bump into walls. When there is a flashlight, i.e., the beginning of healing, the sharp edges are no longer dangerous because you learn to stay away from them. Your flashlight is the *now* and if you miss it, then it is gone forever. Being in the *now*, means being totally in the moment that you are in and recognizing the joy and intensity of that moment.

To sum up, this is a time of dealing with issues of gaining control of your life, facing reality, while dealing simultaneously with feelings of denial interspersed with a great deal of anger. There is anxiety as you try to sort out confusing emotions, events and new roles while denial is something you might still experience. There are fears about the future, not only about how you can cope, but how to go about starting a new life. It is a time of transition.

Denial

While mourning involves the struggle between holding on and letting go, denial keeps you holding on. Denial is no stranger to you as it is a regularly utilized defense that helps to reduce, avoid or prevent anxiety. Denial helps to make life bearable at your time of loss. Denial of loss can take the form of refusing to believe that those we trust may have let us down. It shows up in many ways, such as leaving the deceased's room unchanged, setting an extra place at the table, momentarily believing that you see your loved one in the face of a stranger, avoiding the gravesite, etc.

What does denial look like?

"I felt like I have literally gone crazy," recalls Martha. "I can't remember things; I think my late husband is coming back when the phone or doorbell rings, as though he has only gone somewhere temporarily. I absolutely cannot believe he has died. I can't concentrate very long, although at work I'm fine, but at home or anywhere out of my work environment, I cannot focus."

When death is sudden and unexpected, it can be especially hard to grasp the fact that they are gone. Three months ago Jeanette's husband died suddenly. It happened when she was out of town for two days, a rare event, as they usually traveled together. There was no illness, no warning. "I came home and found his body," says Jeanette. That was on a Sunday and the house was soon filled with paramedics. "I, of course, could only sob; I was literally hysterical." During the days and nights that followed she couldn't eat or sleep, but could only sob. During that first week she stayed with her parents and then they returned home with her. They stayed with her until she decided she needed to be alone in order to get back to her old routine. Despite the overwhelming numbness that had set in, she went back to the gym, called her old therapist, and the following Monday, returned to work.

"I felt secure in my house, so there was no fear of being alone. I have a dog and two cats and, as before, felt that this was my safe place. I was determined to get back to life as I'd known it." A week after her husband's death, she even cooked a Thanksgiving dinner for herself and her parents, something she and her husband had done for years. "Although people were willing to stay with me as long as I needed them to, I couldn't help feeling that they were houseguests. I needed to be alone." Once everyone was gone, she felt relieved not having to put up a false front. "I could finally just let go emotionally. I needed to be alone to give into my pain. I couldn't take care of the people trying to take care of me anymore, including my parents."

She went back to work, where a close friend was particularly loving and supportive, but it was a month before the reality of what had happened began to really sink in. "And then my pain got worse. I was more anxious and had times when I couldn't stop crying." The funeral had been postponed for three weeks because of coroner delays and then Thanksgiving. Being in a kind of limbo was really hard, she said. "The first thing in the morning a part of me still expected to find my husband next to me. Even now, three months later, I still think of all the stuff he used to do and it's really painful." They had talked about making changes to the house, but she's not ready to do it yet. "I haven't even touched his closet.

"My parents have been very supportive, but their attitude is, 'Pick yourself up and move on.' The reality is, no matter how much someone loves me and wants to help, unless they been through this, they can't possibly understand." Her father kept urging her to go forward, forcing her to eventually tell him, "Dad, I'm not you; I don't have to go forward. I just can't do that. I know you mean well, but I have to do this when *I* have to do this." Her father didn't mean to be unkind, but he just didn't know what to say. He kept himself busy around the house, fixing things and trying to take care of his daughter. Both parents, she said, wanted her to feel better but just didn't know what to do.

"My father would ask, 'Do you want to go downstairs and clean out the garage?' I couldn't help but to answer, 'No! The garage is fine!'" Her husband's tools and other possessions were there. It was too hard. "That's why I finally told them I needed to be alone; I needed to get on with my mourning." She found support from the staff at the Neptune Society, but found that most other people would try to help by saying, 'You just have to get over this.' "And I'd answer, 'No, I don't.'"

Her ability to concentrate was nonexistent, even at work. "I remember being in the office, and people telling me what had to be done. After a few minutes I would tell them, 'I didn't hear one word you said.' I was so tired every day." Being an active person who likes to work out helped her release some of the emotion and that terrible energy that had built up inside.

After not having seen her therapist for years, she went in to see her. Ironically the therapist had lost her husband the year before and she encouraged Jeanette to join a weekly bereavement support group. "This group gave structure to my mourning, which made it more manageable." After the first session she didn't want to go again, but the leader asked her to attend three times before making up her mind. "I did and am still there," she said. "There were times when I was so exhausted I didn't want to do anything or go anywhere, but I forced myself," adds Jeannette.

What advice might Jeannette offer others at this stage of her bereavement? Join a support group. Consider private counseling. Try to re-establish your routine, but avoid being so busy that you're not giving yourself time to grieve. "You can keep yourself so frantically busy that you're almost in a denial state and that makes healing even harder," she said. "And do some sort of physical activity, whether it's just walking or working out, or whatever it is that you like to do."

Stay connected with your friends, as well. "Find at least a few friends that you love, friends you can call and be yourself with." But understand, she warns, that friends may not know what to say or do to be helpful. "That's not a bad thing. Try to appreciate that they call, that they send cards. It means that they care."

Jeanette is 41, had been married almost 10 years, but she and her husband had been together for 27. She feels fortunate that she had always had her own independence. "My husband and I were total soul mates, but it wasn't the kind of relationship where we did everything as a couple." At this point she can't envision a time when life will be good again, but there's hope. "Every once in a while I get a glimpse."

Here are several other common denial behaviors: Rose had gone to her best friend's birthday party. Later she was shown pictures of the party and asked, "Where's Bob?" as she searched for her deceased husband. She had temporarily forgotten that he had died. She apologized and her friend understood. While talking about her embarrassment she realized that she was experiencing denial. Then there is Sally, who has to tell herself over and over, "He isn't coming back," recognizing that she goes in and out of this awareness. Jonathan describes his denial as feeling like a dream to him. He intermittently feels that his wife will come back in a few weeks.

Denial lasts as long as it lasts. It is a defense of the ego and designed to protect you until you are ready to move on.

Helpful Do's and Don'ts

Helpful Do's and Don'ts for the Bereaved

Do engage in healing thoughts/feelings.

Do explore healing activities.

Do know it is OK to laugh again.

Do appreciate joy.

Do know you can feel fear and also make progress.

Do know you can feel two kinds of feelings at the same time.

Do know you can say to friends and family, "I'm not ready for that yet."

Do know it's OK not to be perfect.

Do know it's OK to make progress in your own time.

Do participate in community.

Do know that as you help others, you are helping yourself.

Do stay in the moment and enjoy it.

Helpful Do's and Don'ts for
Friends and Family of the Bereaved

Do not tell the bereaved they will be at peace with their loss.

Do not say he/she is in a better place.

Do not say, "It was meant to be."

Do not use cliché expressions which often lack feeling and are disingenuous.

*Please turn to page 251
for the Workbook section on this Time Sequence.*

4.

Time Sequences of Healing Grief
Months Nine through Twelve
Anger

I'M ANGRY. I FEEL like a beached whale. My feelings are huge and flip-flopping all over the place. I thought that I was doing so well, that I would no longer wake each morning crying, that I was finally feeling in control of my life once again. Instead the pain has once again become raw. Sadness overwhelms me. I'm sensitive. I see couples everywhere: walking hand-in-hand on the street, shopping, going to movies. I'm jealous and resentful; sometimes it makes me sad, at other times, angry.

I'm not steady and I don't know what I can count on. My moods are as unpredictable as April weather in New York. March roared and April seemed to be the promise of springtime and daffodils and then the papers reported possible snow. I scarcely understand what I can count on. I bought a raincoat and prepared to get wet. I tried to think about just how many puddles I could avoid. Would I be splashed by drivers turning on flooded street corners unexpectedly? I, who liked to count on definite things, realize the world can't be counted-on to give me what I need. It gave and it took away. I feel like a child wanting my favorite toy back, my train has broken and it cannot be fixed. I can't remember the sound of my husband's voice and that scares me. Friends tell me it's time to donate his clothes to a charity, but I'm afraid to lose his scent.

Yet, some days I do feel confident coming to a year and beyond, thinking that I finally understand the turf. On those days I'm gleeful, hopeful, loving the promise of warm weather, tired of the inner chill — ready to shed my loneliness and sadness, and content to make the most of my life by enjoying time with dear friends and family, even the solitude of curling up with a good book. Other days I realize I haven't yet mastered my healing. Where is my inner guide when I need it the most?

Nights full of longing and nightmares thankfully bring mornings of work and routine. It's easier to handle my structured time, things expected of me, organized in sequences. Easier to be logical than stuck in the quicksand of feelings. But, even with all of this flip-flopping, I am learning how not to sink as low, and learning how to climb out faster. The black hole of emotion is still there, but I now have a ladder to climb out. I call a friend; I take a walk in the park when I need to distract myself from myself. As a child, I prided myself on my inner thought process, a private world which didn't have to be shared ... no one needed to know what I was thinking. Now, I know to seek out a friend, not wanting to be too alone with my thoughts which dwell on my feelings.

Friends encourage me to date; they think it will help, that I won't be so lonely or depressed. But my loneliness has nothing to do with being or not being with other people.

Common Questions

How come I am feeling more depressed now than I was at first?

Waves of depression and anxiety may hit. Is this what my life is going to be like? How will I recover?

Being a third wheel is a major theme; I get many invitations. How shall I choose?

I get torn between wanting to date and staying at home. How will I know when I'm ready?

Am I forgetting my spouse if I begin to date?

Why am I still troubled by uncertainty?

THE NUMBNESS OF shock has worn off and a deep, dark, sadness often pervades your life. Grief is silent-time and in-between time; the time between dusk and daylight; no man's land; an indescribable pain without a painkiller. A numbness that pain transcends ... like having surgery without an anesthetic, an inner rawness that feels like it will never heal. We heal layer by layer and as such, good days are possible, in contrast to the early months when healing didn't even seem possible. But, even now a gentle tap on the top layer of skin can re-awaken earlier pain, for now there is a scar as a reminder.

Why might you be feeling more depressed now than you were at first? In the early months, you are overwhelmed with insurance, paperwork, forms, busy-work and obligations of things to take care of. As time goes on and the veil of early shock lifts, more feelings emerge. As you have more thinking and feeling time, there becomes more time to process the feelings of sadness anger, emptiness, exasperation and frustration. Why did you leave me? Feelings of anger/frustration/depression may surface as an aggitated response for, "I have too many things to take care of and hate it. I am overwhelmed, if you didn't leave, I wouldn't have to face this." Also, as time passes and feelings settle in, your situation and response to it becomes more real; this is permanent, he or she is not coming back. Waves of depression and anxiety may hit. In your state of depression, you may be thinking: "Is this what my life is going to be like? How will I recover?"

Yet, in contrast, while you don't want to forget your beloved; the memories begin to grow dimmer. The voice, the scent of the beloved will be less acute, like a bright light that fades. And it must, in order to illuminate other rooms yet to be discovered. In holding on, some want the photograph to never fade; as they pass by the picture, they will kiss it, touch it or speak to it ... not implying that life doesn't end, but just recognizing how hard it is to deal with death. You wonder how to seek recovery, to return to normalcy, while at the same time, feeling that the world will never be "normal" again.

Living with Yourself

If I have known you for 50 years, how do I now sleep alone in our bed? How do I turn over and you are not there? How do I sleep with an empty pillow, an empty place where you used to lie? How do I adjust to that when I don't want to and what does "adjustment" really mean? Does it require that I accept losing you? How do I do that? If I say "yes" to my first date — am I moving forward even if I want him to leave when he takes me home? I'm quasi ready to be a friend and nothing more. There is still a wasteland around my heart, a snowstorm of bewilderment and the north wind to blow me away.

If I thought I knew loneliness before, it now has a new face. When I wasn't looking, someone else inhabited my body. I don't recognize myself, I am a record caught in a groove and so I play it over and over again. Even I am getting weary of the repeated refrain. I want a new tune, yet I'm not quite ready for it. Sometimes I think about getting the piano tuned or the harp re-strung. I need a new instrument or a major overhaul of the old one but I still want to recognize its face. I will not abandon my old violin. It's as if I am a fine old antique but I can't locate the polish to make me shine.

And, yet, during this time of "flip-flopping" emotion, the music changes and you learn a new song. It's as if you re-discover the piano and that your fingers can roam over the keys and play sweet music. You no longer want the comfort of your dark feelings, and you welcome the sunshine, the morning, the aroma of coffee. You even notice your chenille robe, rubbing your fingers over its texture, no longer oblivious to your surroundings. You are becoming healthy! You have more energy and notice that your garden needs attending. You want to clip back the dead roses and encourage new growth. The clouds lift and you look forward to tomorrow.

One day you are ready to begin again, the next day the pain of loss is truly felt, endless memories triggered by seemingly trivial events. If, as for most people life is a complex web of relationships, then the death of a spouse cuts an uncountable number of threads in that web. What becomes clear is how deeply the now severed threads have been intertwined into your life. Yet, as author Simcha Paull Raphael (*Jewish View of the Afterlife*, Jason Aronson, Pub.) points out so beautifully, "As a knot appears unexpectedly in a thread, so deft strokes can untangle it and life continues evenly. But if it cannot be corrected, then it must be quietly woven into a new design. Thus, the finished piece can still be beautiful — even though not as perfect as planned."

As the first anniversary (of the death) approaches, however, there is also a heightened awareness that social and family events must now be faced alone.

Marjanie's husband Myron passed away nine months ago. "He had been gravely ill for a short time," says Marjanie, "and although I thought I was prepared, I discovered that I was not. He was a humorous and lively man, and he was my hero. Myron was nineteen years older than me, but he was young at heart. We did everything together, the simple things that many couples do. We respected each other, we enjoyed each other's company and we enjoyed our own space too. When I needed advice I would ask Myron. Sometimes I didn't like his answer, but I listened. The emptiness I felt after his death is hard to explain. It was physical and mental. The ache in my chest was real, although my brain would try to convince me otherwise. However, I did know that I would need a support group to deal with the loneliness I felt.

"I did not attend an official bereavement support group. My husband and I had a very close relationship with several couples. We would go out to dinner every weekend, attend parties, social events, and sporting events together. The first weekend after I buried my husband, the 'group' invited me to dinner. At first I refused. I felt awkward and uncomfortable and even a little guilty about having a good time when I should be grieving. Then after much soul searching, I went out to dinner with my friends, and have continued this practice. These people have been my support group. Since my husband had a tendency to be opinionated, many of his views have lingered with us. His name generally comes up in a conversation as well as his viewpoint. The first time we talked about him it was difficult, but I have learned to enjoy the memories we shared as a group. I have also learned to make the adjustment to being single within a gathering of couples.

"My greatest fear was facing the holidays alone. Everyone would always come to our house for holiday meals. Myron had children from a previous marriage, so we never were a slave to a 'date.' He enjoyed spending time with his boys and his grandchildren whenever their schedules would allow. This year, my sister moved to Florida. She invited me to spend the winter with her and her husband, so I took them up on their offer. I had also retired from my job and was now able to refocus my energies. It was the best thing that happened to me. This year everyone came to my sister's house and I helped her with the entertaining. The most difficult holiday was New Year's Eve. It brought back memories of cheers of good health and happiness but again friends as well as family made the transition to 2006 a little easier.

"I do think that if a person tries to deal with the death of a spouse alone they are making a serious mistake. I had the luxury of a network of close friends and family. I also forced myself to keep 'busy.' I hate the term, but keeping the mind and body occupied is a necessary part of the healing process. I also was lucky enough to meet many new friends along the way. I still miss my husband very much. I miss him every time I have dinner alone ... the quiet is deafening. I miss him holding me at night ... the bed seems too big now. I miss him making me laugh ... with his bad jokes and hokey puns. I miss him making love to me ... his kisses, his touch, his smell. I will always miss him. He was my first love. He stole my heart and took a piece of it with him when he died."

Anxieties

Should I attend social events if invited? How should I handle discussion (or lack of discussion) about my husband or wife? If the event is in my immediate family, e.g. graduation, children's marriage, birth of a grandchild, should I attend the event or celebration? Can I celebrate and mourn at the same time? How do I avoid "breaking down" near others? For those who are Jewish, there is the unveiling of the grave marker, a traditional, but not obligatory, ceremony carried out at a time before the first anniversary. At the unveiling, all the issues at this state of mourning can present themselves with inexorable harshness.

"I've been told that this ceremony marks the end of mourning. I don't feel that way. In fact, I feel worse than at the beginning. Why?" If the unveiling of the grave marker, as well as the period between Thanksgiving and New Year's Day take place during this time sequence of mourning, it can be especially difficult. Due to your new, full awareness of your loss, it can be devastating. Thanksgiving Day emphasizes the gathering together of families. Whatever the religious content of Christmas, etc., they too are family celebrations. New Year's Day is often a time to take stock, assessing the past and planning the future. All of these activities can seem to become empty, painful charades.

"What future is there for me beyond the feeling of unending, unchanging desolation?" It is so very important to be part of a bereavement support group as members share specific tactics and strategies of what worked for them. Scheduling in advance for difficult days and events is often helpful. Make plans to spend time with family, with old friends or new friends, travel, or for some, spend time alone by choice. No one tactic works for everyone nor does one tactic work every time but they are options to consider.

Hope
Yet, amid the themes of loss and sadness, joy, freedom and hope can be felt. Everyone reading this book is part of a group of diverse human beings, joined together by a stunning loss, but not all are at the same stage. Some of you have gone through the "crash with reality" and

beyond; some have bypassed it. It cannot be repeated too often that each of you goes through grief, mourning and healing in a unique way, the differences as important as the similarities. Not only are mourners diverse from one another, you are diverse within yourself, sad and joyous, your changeable moods surprising you with breath-taking velocity. The strengths of belonging to a support group are made evident as those, now joyless, can hear from those who have passed through a difficult phase and find some pleasures and satisfactions in their lives.

Progress through mourning is not simply one of stages that automatically follow one after another, each better than the one before. Rather, it is like an intricately choreographed dance where steps forward and steps backward come in tumbling succession; at any given moment one is not sure that any progress has been made. One suggestion is to compare where you are now with the self you remember of three months ago, six months ago, and at the beginning. This focus gives you a span in which you can acknowledge change.

Dating

Being a third wheel is a major theme. "I get many invitations. How shall I choose?" "Should I accept that wedding invitation? I hate going to weddings alone. It will bring up loneliness and a reminder that I am alone. I hate to face these events myself. I will go in my own car and leave early … I don't want to sit at the table alone when everyone else is dancing…"

And it is now when muted thoughts about dating burst into full force. While men often date sooner than women, "How will I know when I'm ready? Is it too soon? Am I forgetting my spouse if I begin dating? What will my children say? Why am I hesitating and troubled by uncertainty?" Be aware that this very uncertainty may be a reflection of your changing perspectives about yourself. But, it is important to trust that you will know when you are ready to act.

The turmoil about re-entering the social world, and re-dating again as a single person, resembles nothing so much as adolescence revisited. "I get torn between wanting to date and staying at home." There might be anger at being in the position of dating again, but, there is also hope at the promise of adventure. Your future begins to emerge from this changing perception of yourself.

Dating begins to bring in social elements that help you enjoy your life again. Wanting to go out is normal and acceptable but the ego might not be ready. It is helpful to realize that you can contain both feelings. Honor the feeling of exploration in the world and wanting to be loyal to your spouse. It is important to know that while you give yourself permission to enjoy life again and go on, you may still be mired in the past, even with a dedication to stay there. It is a literal struggle for movement. It is okay to honor both feelings, and yes, still move forward. Literally, you have to give yourself permission to enjoy your life again and your work is about feeling less guilty over moving forward.

The World In Between

"When you suffer the loss of a spouse, you embark on the difficult, lonely journey of grieving. Somewhere in the process of grieving and healing, you will move through the 'world in-between,'" says Dr. Christner. "You might be thinking, 'What is the world in-between? It must be a mistake. I'm not supposed to be here ... but yet, I am. It no longer feels like my world.' Everything is changed ... hopes, dreams, lifestyles, aspirations, family, friends ... the life that you once knew is suddenly gone. Life no longer seems familiar, no longer feels comfortable, no longer is the one that you knew and created.

"There are so many changes, both externally and internally. One of my group members once said 'I feel like I'm living in a parallel universe since my husband died. I'm over here watching everyone else live life.' Suddenly, you feel like a 'stranger in a strange land,' living in a twilight place. The 'world in-between' can be a confusing, painful and disorienting place. It's a place that must be visited between an ending and a new beginning, between feeling hopeless and finding hope; between loss and beginning a changed life.

"This is the place of transition, the place between an ending and a beginning, the place of being lost and of finding, of re-identifying and re-inventing, the place of healing through grief and learning to integrate that your world has changed forever and will begin again. It will never be the same: but you will begin again. The book, *The Way of Transition: Embracing Life's Most Difficult Moments* (Perseus Publishing) by William Bridges offers guidelines and knowledge for traveling through the 'world in-between.' Although he had written several other books and had been an authority on transition at a corporate level for many years, he best began to understand it as he went through his own grief process after the loss of his wife to cancer. After her death, this book was written from his personal experience and journey through his transition through and to his changed life. Although his works apply to transition during any kind of loss, not just the death of a loved one, I will use some of his ideas to specifically address the loss of a spouse.

"According to Mr. Bridges, there are 'four cardinal aspects of the experience of loss.' Using some of Mr. Bridges thoughts, as well as my own, I will briefly explain and give examples of these concepts.

"1. 'Disengagement' – There is a separation from your spouse through death. This separation occurs on many levels: physically, emotionally and mentally. It does not mean that you will forget.

"2. 'Dis-identification' – There are changes in your identity, the 'you' that you used to be. You're no longer the person or the roles that you used to feel, believe or live. 'If I'm no longer a wife/husband/caregiver, then who am I?'

"3. 'Disenchantment' – There are changes in your once familiar life. Suddenly, you are disillusioned because you no longer are living in the reality that you once knew.

"4. 'Disorientation' – After losing your spouse and familiar aspects of your life and "you", you feel confused, disoriented and lost.

"As Mr. Bridges grieved and healed through the death of his wife, he added what he believed to be two additional aspects of loss:

"5. 'Discovery' – You begin to realize and find that you have a new perspective, a new identity and a new life.

"6. 'Disloyalty' – Discovering that you and your life has changed and can actually feel meaningful and good again may cause you to feel that you are being disloyal to your deceased spouse.

"As you go through these stages of transition, you will begin to find light and to heal. It is normal to have loss. It is normal to grieve. It is normal to begin again. That is the way of life. I offer a few suggestions to help you through the process of grief/transition and healing.

"1. If your grief is complicated, seek professional help from a licensed therapist.

"2. Read books that will educate, support, bring comfort and inspire. Recommendations are available.

"3. Having a transitional object, something that belonged to your spouse (i.e. ring, shirt, socks, picture, and key chain) can bring comfort during a time when nothing seems to bring comfort. It's ok to carry it with you, to touch it, to remember.

"4. Talk to yourself in a way that serves to perpetuate healing. The way you talk to yourself can make a difference. If you can, keep your thoughts in the present moment. Read inspirational thoughts that give you support and comfort. It's too easy to feel hopeless and predict the worst by going into the future. It's not here yet ... and you will change. Determining what the future holds will only reflect the pain that you feel now.

"5. Having the belief that you can survive this loss and heal will help to bring hope, courage and something to hold on to. Some people find that their religion and faith give them support. Seek beliefs that support your healing and recovery.

"6. Grieving is an individual journey. Making comparisons or judging yourself against others will not assist you in your healing. Trust that, with the support of others, you will heal ... in your own unique way, in your own unique time.

"7. Do seek support through friends, family and support groups. Being in a support group with others who are on a similar journey can give comfort and reassurance during this difficult time.

"8. Give yourself the time that you need to grieve and to heal. Sometimes you need to visit the grief. Sometimes you need to visit the distractions and resources in your life. Allow room for both. It's the 'space in–between' where the healing begins. I want to remind you that grieving, transition and healing are a process, not an event.

"It will take as long as it takes for you to travel this journey. You won't do it 'wrong.' You will do it the way that you need to to heal. Statistically, it is believed that normal, healthy, uncomplicated grieving takes about two years. For some individuals, it will be shorter and for others, longer. Trust YOUR progress and your journey. Trust that you, too, will heal. Trust that you will find life and light again. My loving thoughts and heart go with you on your most difficult journey. I believe in you and your ability to heal," concludes Dr. Christner.

Freedom to Be You

You may not have been aware of how a relationship permeated your life until that relationship ended. Now, in the midst of loss, you may rediscover freedom, options considered and choices made without the mediating voice of your absent partner. Whether in small decisions about movies, concerts, or restaurants, in large decisions about houses and relocations, or all the decisions in between, the same instant that brings this sense of an absent voice also brings you the sense that you are free to choose. You may indulge yourself, or take actions that would have been judged as frivolous or unwise in the past. This freedom may be unwanted, even unacknowledged, but it is there.

Inner Trust

"Why am I troubled by uncertainty?" Trusting one's inner core is an important part of your healing, yet uncertainty is the expected feeling to this loss; trial and error, entering into the world, testing the waters inch-by-inch are all part of adjustment. The uncertainty may reflect changing perceptions of your 'self.' However, your inner self will give you guidance as to when to act. It's okay to feel conflicted; we all do when the see-saw of emotion is a big part of our day to day life. Energy shifts; sometimes we hold our feelings down, and sometimes we let them go.

Know that it is okay to move forward. It is okay to feel anger, recognize it, and yet, choose life, movement, energy and survival.

Anger—Directed Outward and Inward

When denial can no longer be maintained, feelings of anger, rage, envy and resentment may show up. This anger may be directed outward or inward. Anger toward yourself may look like self-blame, (i.e., "I should have done more ... If only I had ...") resulting in feelings of guilt, shame, helplessness and fear. When directed outward, there is a danger of becoming caught up in bitterness, resentment and alienation. Instead of feeling the normal grieving feelings of sorrow and emotional pain, you may lash out at any convenient scapegoat (i.e., the doctors, God, an inept salesperson, etc.). When you admit your anger to yourself, talk to someone you trust. It is important to work through your feelings of anger and fear, as well as feelings of guilt and envy.

Few survivors escape without some feeling of guilt. You might feel guilty because you did not make sure your spouse took care of his or her health or got to the doctor sooner. Or, you gave permission for surgery and your spouse didn't recover or you arranged for your spouse to be taken off life support systems. A long illness may have led to a feeling of resentment and consequently guilt over that resentment. A sudden or accidental death may give rise to the torture of all kinds of "if only's."

A common emotion, yet difficult to face, is envy at a world that seems full of couples, people that can plan trips, buy season tickets for the theatre, go out to dinner, etc., knowing they will always have their spouse to accompany them. It may manifest itself as anger or suddenly hit like a ton of bricks long past the anger and immediate-mourning stage, at a time when you are seemingly picking up the pieces of your life and moving ahead. Before the death, you thought that you knew what the rest of your life would look like and that has now forever changed.

The state of anger may be very difficult for friends and family to cope with, because this anger is aimed in all directions, including at yourself. Be aware that anger is an integral, normal part of grief and needs to be addressed before you can move on.

Anger Directed Outward

"My husband died five months ago and at this point, I actually find my anger motivating," said Carole. "My relationship with my husband's family, except for a few people, has been very difficult for the past 14 years." Their anger and antagonism toward her had been going on for years and came to the surface full-force immediately after her husband's death. Fortunately, Carole had the support of her two sons, a daughter and her brother.

"While I am in touch with feeling some anger at my late husband, mostly I am angry at his family." Before he died, Carole had always hoped to fix the problems in the family, but now realized that would never happen. "That part of my life died when I buried my husband. I have decided that if his family can't be loving and supportive, then I don't need them in my life anymore, with the exception of a niece, nephew, and sister-in-law from that side." There's a certain relief in having chosen who, in her late husband's family she will deal with, she said.

During the marriage, Carole's husband was morbidly obese, a condition which contributed to his death. "And I'm angry at that." Two weeks before he passed away he told her he knew he was dying, but she couldn't accept it. "He even took me to the cemetery while he took care of all the arrangements for his funeral, so he was still taking care of everyone but himself and I'm still angry about that."

Her husband, Carole said, was an intelligent man who knew what he was doing to his health and should have stopped doing it. But at the same time, she acknowledges,

"He was such a sweet and good person, and I don't want to be angry ... it's very hard to have anger at someone who, at the time, tried to do the best that he could."

She's also angry at herself. "How do I express that anger? I cry. When I'm alone I talk out loud to him. I tell him about the family situation and what has happened." She has accepted that that part of her life is gone, "And it is up to me to try to remember the good parts and let go of the bad parts."

And yet, anger can be a motivating force for good. Now, Carole is making her own choices, taking care of herself physically by maintaining a weight loss she achieved several years ago, for instance, instead of filling herself up emotionally by overeating. "I took my anger and tried to use it as a force for good in my life and the lives of my children. And I can now say that instead of being someone's daughter- or sister-in-law, I have become the mother in my own family."

Anger basically has two directions — outward or inward. Turned outward in healthy grief, it is universally and inevitably directed against the lost partner, even when that person is lost through death. Anger toward your late spouse stems from two sources: previous hostility present in the relationship, and hostility at that person for dying and leaving you potentially helpless and abandoned. When anger is expressed outwardly, you commonly project it on other people — anyone who is not suffering in the same way you are. Anger can also be directed toward people who attempt to be comforting because to accept such comfort is a reminder of the loss and triggers yet more pain.

Loss can bring forth another type of anger. There are some people who handle uncomfortable feelings by denying them and lashing out at any convenient scapegoat. Because these feelings are part of grief, you might find yourself "snapping" at others instead of feeling sorrow or pain.

The danger to projecting anger onto others is that you may become caught up in bitterness, resentment, and alienation. After admitting your anger to yourself, talk to someone you trust. This may be frightening, but anger accumulates and will erupt eventually, maybe frightening or hurting another person. A good friend may be a good listener or a professional therapist may help you work through your feelings of anger or fear.

When anger builds up to the point of explosion, there are techniques for letting off steam without hurting yourself or others. Pent-up emotions are stored in the body and can be released through physical activity: screaming or beating on a pillow, tearing up a telephone book or even throwing stones in the ocean can be helpful. So too are taking long walks, working out in a gym, or swimming. Less physical outlets might include talking into a tape recorder, writing in a personal journal or drawing pictures that express your feelings. These activities often provide temporary relief by releasing pent-up feelings.

Anger Directed Inward

Anger directed inward, can result in illness. Sherry admittedly had a lot of difficult family issues before her husband passed away. She had a full-time, stressful job, a grown daughter living at home, and other problems that were escalating out of control. While this was happening, she was not aware that her husband had an illness he was keeping secret. "Leading up to my husband's illness, we had a lot of family issues. I was angry at myself because I did not behave in a manner that was acceptable to me. I didn't realize what shape I was in until one day I slashed my wrists. Two months later, I found out that my husband was going to die." Had she known, she would have sought help for herself sooner. Instead, she could only feel remorse and guilt that the person she had loved all her life hadn't let her know that he was sick.

Sherry's husband had been a loving, supportive and introspective person before becoming ill, but afterward, his behavior changed drastically. To cope, Sherry would withdraw into crossword puzzles and other solitary distractions. "After his death I learned to reel myself in emotionally, and have since become more mellow." But feelings of guilt lingered on. "I didn't feel as if I had been as kind, caring or as good as I should have been, whether he was sick or not. Now that he's gone I feel a great loneliness." From previous counseling she had learned to step back and remind herself that her husband cared, that he understood, and loved her anyway. "I can still hear his, 'Aw, babe' in my head. We had the kind of relationship that allowed us to be in the same room, each doing something different, and still be touching each other emotionally.

Sometimes Sherry is still angry at herself, thinking, What if I had done more? Why didn't I question his weight loss? "The guilt is still there because I miss him so much."

Sonia, a widow for almost three years, recalls the challenge of accepting that she was no longer part of a couple. "I was on my own. It was like my husband and I had been riding on a beautiful flying carpet, and then, when he died the carpet was pulled out from under me and I fell to earth."

During their marriage, Sonia's husband had taken complete and expert charge of all the family's finances, and even though Sonia had asked to participate and become knowledgeable, her husband's response was always, 'Absolutely not!' Like so many others in her situation, when she was on her own she didn't know where to start.

"Although now I'm doing fine, the transition was slow and painful. It was like I slammed into a brick wall. I was aware that we owned an apartment house (which we didn't live in) with ten families dependent upon our managing it well. I slowly tried to find out all that was involved in taking care of the apartments and the tenants within." To her surprise, she found that dealing with the tenants was much easier for her than it had been for her husband, Joe, because he had been an introvert. "Dealing with people disturbed his inner peace, but I am an extrovert and I feel that interacting with people makes my life richer."

At first, Sonia had no one to teach her the ropes of taking care of the apartment or her personal finances. Because she had been raised by an independent mother, she had learned a lot of things, but not how to delegate responsibility. "So for the first six months, I wrestled with everything on my own. And, because of my overwhelming sadness it was doubly hard." Slowly, she came out of her sadness, and was able to reach out and find an accountant and other help that she needed.

"Also, thank God, I had a business background, first as a teacher before retirement, and then as a paralegal, after going back to school at UCLA. I had managed my life pretty well, except I'd always had a partner, my husband. Almost three years later I still miss Joe, I still miss our marriage, I miss our life, but I feel pretty self-sufficient in my life now."

Nonetheless, she felt a betrayal when her husband died because she had always viewed him as a survivor. "He was a bright, fine, very good man, who had spent the war years in Siberia with his mother, father, and his sister." The rest of the family perished in the Holocaust in Germany. And while Sonia admired Joe tremendously, the reality was that he was not an optimist. He always lived with a certain amount of anxiety and pessimism. "For example, when he turned 67 he had a major heart attack and was supposed to have heart bypass surgery. He did not want to do it." His daughters begged, and finally Joe told them that he didn't want an angiogram, a prelude to surgery. "I asked him why and he said that it would be ridiculous to die from an angiogram."

Finally, with the help of the doctor, Joe was convinced to have the angiogram, but still balked at surgery. So they went step-by-step.

"When the only option left was surgery, he declined saying he wished to die. So, yes, I was angry. I felt entitled to have him remain by my side." When there were no more options, Joe finally had his surgery at age 67. Now, fast forward to the age of 73. He had gone through cardiac rehabilitation and remained alive, but was very angry. He really wanted to die. "Those five years were a struggle," Sonia said, "but we had them. Then he told me, 'I've given you five years, I don't wish to be on this diet anymore, I'm really a couch potato, and I don't wish to exercise or walk, or do anything I don't want to do.' So I said, fine, thank you for the five years. I'm going to take a walk."

The next day Joe was in a good mood. In the morning, Sonia and he had a cup of coffee together and she asked him if he wanted to go for a walk. "He turned to me and said, 'I came from Siberia to California to meet my bride, Sonia, and now that I've met her, she's going to take a walk!' And I said, thank you for the nice poetry, I'll be back between 1 and 1:15. He said, 'Fine. Have a nice walk.' I took my walk, came back and found him on the floor. He had had a cerebral hemorrhage. He had told me that he wanted to die in such a way that he wouldn't be aware of it. And he did."

Sonia's anger manifested in asthma attacks. She also felt depressed, and when she told a consulting psychiatrist her story, he said her anger was justified. "From time to time I still get very sad, but I have many interests, lovely daughters and friends," she said. "I am hopeful that life will be fruitful, that I can make a contribution, and find out what it is that God put me here for."

Anger can come slowly, or be felt immediately, as was Jill's experience: Like Sonia, Jill was also angry at her dead spouse for becoming overweight and not taking good care of himself. She was upset, too, about his family, that he helped them excessively while letting his own welfare slide. Her anger extends to what she considers lost opportunities and times in her life that held promise and are now gone. She is learning to take responsibility for the 'Now,' to look less at what was done to her and more at what she participated in. She is not only angry at him, she is angry at herself for the lost possibilities of what she could have become.

Unexpressed anger is anger turned inward and repressed. The result can be depression, nightmares, psychosomatic and organic disorders, accompanied by ruminations about the dreadful past, or even suicide. Anger turned against yourself complicates your completion of mourning. It is important to understand that underneath anger is fear. Fear of meeting your own needs, of making decisions, fear that you won't be able to manage financially, emotionally, and physically.

While you may feel guilt over feeling angry at your late spouse, ultimately, healthy mourning requires that anger must be expressed against the lost loved one in order for you to move ahead in your healing.

Helpful Do's and Don'ts

Helpful Do's and Don'ts for the Bereaved

Do recognize depression when you can't get out of bed, eat or sleep.

Do know it is OK to ask for help when depressed; friends and family may not be enough.

Do know it is OK to say no to an invitation. You may not feel like going to an event.

Do take your own car so you can leave when you wish.

Do know it is acceptable to feel more depressed now than in the beginning. You are defrosting, so more feelings are surfacing.

Do know you won't forget but the memories will be less painful.

Do know recovery is possible; people heal when they let themselves.

Do know that it is possible to make steps forward and then some steps backwards.

Helpful Do's and Don'ts for Friends and Family of the Bereaved

Don't always insist that you have to pay for dinner, allow the bereaved to reciprocate.

Don't tell them not to feel like a "third wheel," they do.

Don't tell them you know how it feels for them, you don't.

Don't make assumptions about the bereaved unless you have been bereaved.

Don't tell them to "move on;" they cannot until they are ready.

Don't assume you understand what they feel.

Don't tell them to sell the house, "it's too big." "Why do you need such a big place?"

Don't push friends too hard. They have their own sense as to when they are ready.

Please turn to page 282
for the Workbook section on this Time Sequence.

5.

Time Sequences of Healing Grief
Months Thirteen through Seventeen
Depression

INSTEAD OF THINKING *only in terms of my grief, on some days summer breezes slowly begin to beckon. I've learned the world is not a perfect place. I break glasses when I'm clumsy; I bruise myself if I move too fast and walk into the edges of rooms. But, I have let my rooms expand. I have discarded what I do not need. I have given away his clothing and some of my feelings of depression. I have scaled down. I have embraced the lightness. I have opened the windows to drink in fresh air.*

I have dreamed of open meadows and flower fields, picked wild daisies and gathered arms full of fragrant lilacs. I snipped pink rose buds for my vases and I danced alone in my house to music. I have prepared balanced meals, and did not neglect the vegetables. I brewed tea leaves in exotic flavors. I lit candles and hummed. I welcomed guests into my home and delighted again in preparing gourmet meals.

It felt as if I had spent a long winter in Cape Cod, and now I badly needed sun and light ... needed the curtains to blow in the breeze; needed to shed a thousand layers of doubt; needed to see the world as a friendly place, filled with people. I no longer welcomed my aloneness; nor did I want to settle for it. I wanted my nature to be true and return to me. I wanted company when I took a walk, wanted to hold hands in a movie. I wanted to enter the world of the living. I applauded my own return.

I moved through mourning. I walked straight ahead with focus and purpose. It didn't matter how fast I walked – what mattered was that I made slow, steady progress and I had made it across the bridge. When I looked back, I was surprised at my amazing journey. Like an outsider, I watched myself progress without judgment. I could see that small steps were sufficient; I could not run across to my destination. I felt blessed that I was whole, not empty, not missing any limbs – and so different from the earlier me, when I had felt my heart wrenched out of me and my throat always parched. Instead, I felt rejuvenated and joyful. I was totally involved in the experience of healing, not an outsider looking in.

Common Questions

What will the rest of my life be like?

Will I ever have love in my life again?

How can I set a long term goal when I'm not even sure of a short term goal?

Am I going to be able to live alone the rest of my life if I don't reconnect?

I moved from my parents' home to a marriage. How can I do everything by myself alone?

On the days I feel overwhelmed, what strategies should I employ?

How do I help myself get energy?

How do I get to feel hopeful that life will hold promise?

What part do I have to play in making my life better?

CERTAIN THEMES EMERGE during these months of mourning. For many people the second year of mourning is more painful than the first. In the beginning, the psyche is protected. Otherwise, you would be overwhelmed with all kinds of feelings. In the beginning, emotions are frozen, and as time goes on, they begin to thaw. This seems to be nature's way of protecting you. As your emotions continue to return, you may experience sadness on an ever deeper level, a sadness that replaces the initial impact of loss and devastation. Be assured, however, that despite your current pain, there is significant growth and forward movement as you adapt to being alone.

Shifting Emotions
While you may be ready to begin thinking about and setting some long-term goals, the opposite may also be true. You may still be struggling with the here and now. In the early part of mourning, you were encouraged to participate in life on a "one day at a time" basis as a coping strategy.

But now there is a back and forth motion to mourning and healing. You may wake up depressed, and then as the day progresses, feel better. Or, you may feel happy in the morning, and then, sad. Your range of emotions in the course of any one day may still vary quite a bit. Likened to the game of Monopoly®, some days you will move three squares forward and two back. At other times, you will move more back than forward. Some days you'll land on "Chance" or "Free Parking." This is all normal.

Triggers may be memories, dreams, music, photographs, movies, family events, holidays, or anything at all. Much like a young child learning to walk as he takes one step forward, falls, picks himself up and takes off again, so goes your healing. Just like the child, however, each time that you pick yourself up you become stronger and gain more confidence in your ability to create a new and rewarding life for yourself.

Some days you might still find yourself thinking, "Is this all there is?" and, "Am I going to spend the rest of my life lonely?" It is important to recognize the difference between being alone and being lonely. Some of you may finally be able and willing to explore new areas of your life and emotions as you have healed from the inside out. But the layers of wounding take time to heal and the process cannot be rushed. Each of you has your own timetable, and so, *healing takes as long as it takes*. We have offered you guideposts to help you along the path of mourning and healing, but no one can provide a script.

We offer this analogy to surgery. After a patient has had a surgical procedure, we expect it to take time to heal. Actually, the inner layers heal first, from inside to outside. However, after a loss, people sometimes are inclined to hurry the process, thinking to avoid some of the pain. Unfortunately that doesn't work, nor does time itself heal. *Healthy* healing takes time and work.

Sometimes you might have trouble expressing your feelings of sadness and are tempted to cover them up with inappropriate laughter. However, think ... When there is inappropriate laughter, what is the laughter covering up, what is making you so uncomfortable right now that you are making jokes?

"When should I send out thank you notes for sympathy cards? When should I take off my ring?" The only viable answer is, when it feels right for you. We encourage you not to be locked into a specific timetable, but rather to listen to your inner voice.

At this time you also might be focusing on the ramifications of your loss, your expectations of feeling better, your continued guilt in regard to dating, your ambivalence of feelings and riding the waves of emotional upheaval. By this time you might have *expected* to be feeling better, and you are not. You might not have been prepared for reliving your loss. And then, between 13 to 17 months, reality hits. You expected to feel better but instead have a profound sense of sadness. Yet, in a matter of weeks, it is entirely possible to find this emotional depression lifting.

Ongoing Guilt

You may still be feeling guilt in terms of proceeding on with your own life. You may still be troubled and anxious over the prospect of socialization again with a new partner. Having a good time on a date often produces feelings of ambivalence. "How can I enjoy myself when my spouse isn't here?" Survivor's guilt? It is all right to enjoy life again and we continue to encourage you to give permission to yourself to experience whatever you are feeling; feelings are neither right or wrong, they are just feelings ... and they are yours. Try not to be judgmental about how you feel on any given day.

If and when you do begin to date, do keep in mind that another relationship is not a substitute for the grieving and healing process. Be careful about thinking that everything is "better now." Overlapping grieving and loving is not unusual. It is important that you continue to attend your bereavement support group, to continue to grieve while sorting out this "new life."

Be heartened, you are rounding the bend of recovery even though you may still be feeling some form of depression.

Depression

Anger turned inward also becomes depression. Depression often manifests itself as feelings of helplessness and being overwhelmed. It is the result of dealing with a new and unwanted life-change and expecting yourself to manage your daily obligations and emotions as you did when your loved one was alive. Seek help where and when needed and acknowledge every success, no matter how small. When the depression is not dealt with, the grieving process is delayed. Often it is helpful to speak with a therapist or counselor for assistance in dealing with these overwhelming feelings.

Geri's husband died 17 months ago, and yet, sometimes when her mind drifts and she's driving home, for instance, she'll find herself daydreaming that her husband will be there waiting. "It makes me sad all over again when I realize that it's not true." Her house is close to the street with a picture window and she imagines him there, sitting on the couch waiting for her when she drives up. "It's not that I consciously think that he'll be there, but...

"I have never felt angry at him, just at the situation." She's angry about the big things and even the little things – having to pay bills and work on the house – problems her husband routinely handled. "So I feel angry inside, although I don't throw things or anything like that." To deal with her depression she does a lot of walking and still takes a low-dose antidepressant her doctor prescribed because, in the beginning, she couldn't stop crying.

"It was always unacceptable for me to cry in public, although I would cry a lot at home. I didn't mind crying in my grief support group and with close friends, but not with some of my other friends who just didn't know how to respond to my ongoing sadness and depression." She feared that if she were always sad, they wouldn't want her around, even though they weren't sending any such signals. "This was something I projected on them, because that's probably how I would react if somebody I recently met were always sad and depressed and needy. I know that I would not want to be around them."

Geri is aware that her depression has made her extremely sensitive. "Anytime something doesn't go my way, or something bad happens, it becomes magnified ten thousand times. Like if I was to get a flat tire, I'd just sit down and cry for twenty minutes." Her ability to cope, even with smaller difficulties or frustrations, is nonexistent, she said. To compensate, she tries to take care of herself by sleeping until 9 a.m., even though she had risen at 5 a.m. through her entire working life. "Sleeping late makes the day shorter," and for Geri, the most stressful time of the day is morning.

The most challenging aspect of her mourning is trying to function and fight depression. She has become suspicious and untrusting so that even ordinary tasks, such as having work done on her home, seem filled with peril. She resents having to stay home waiting for workmen, and when they get there, she doesn't trust them.

"In the beginning I wanted to meet another man right away, to rescue me. And I went to social events to try to meet somebody. Nothing happened and it was devastating. I went with a friend to a dance and no one asked me to dance."

In her depression, she thought that if she could only find another man, the world would 'right itself' again. Now, even that unrealistic hope has faded and the depression continues. "I'm convinced that I will never be a whole person again, a realization that came to me after the first year of mourning. I came to the conclusion that this is how my life is now." Geri and her husband had enjoyed an extremely blissful relationship, she said. They had no children, and their lives were wrapped around each other. "I will never meet anybody like that again," she said. "I was the only important thing in his life.

"To compromise and settle for a lesser relationship is out of the question. I still want to be the most important person in a man's life, but there are certain things that I'm just not willing to do to have a man." Things she sees other people doing in order to have a partner, things she wouldn't consider. "It would be nice to know that somebody would still find me attractive though. And that hasn't happened yet. This is how it is; this is how my life is now."

Yet, it is important to note that happiness is a relative term. It is a by-product of all else. If one is living their life fully, attending events they love and enjoy, participating in the world, going to the movies, theatre, travel, etc. they may recognize that they are happy. But, as happy as they were before their spouse died, some feel that this part has forever been taken away. Others may feel more joy, more appreciation. When we define our entire world with one person and then that person is gone, the world feels empty.

In Geri's view, not having children doesn't make life harder or lonelier, because in her view, grown children have their own lives, which don't change much when a parent dies. "The reality is that losing a parent is not the same as losing a spouse," she said. "I've lost my today and my tomorrows. But I feel better knowing this. I don't have the highs and the lows, just a kind of moderate low all the time, without expectations. In a way that has really helped me."

Probably the most common form of hopelessness is depression, from which millions of people suffer. There are major differences, however, between bereavement and clinical depression.

What does this difference look like? When we are bereaved, despite our sadness, we can laugh and show a variety of emotions appropriate to what is going on around us at any given moment. For example, you might laugh at the antics of an infant even in the midst of grief. People suffering from clinical depression remain downcast regardless of what is going on about them. In our grieving, we can still respond to reassurance, support, and comfort. We also retain the capacity for pleasure while feeling depressed over what has been lost.

Our temporary symptoms of bereavement depression and those of ongoing clinical depression can however look the same, including irritability, insomnia, eating too much or not enough, difficulty getting out of bed, lack of motivation, loss of self esteem, feeling as if you are under a dark cloud, and perhaps, feeling a heaviness in your chest. Depression can also manifest itself as feeling worthless, a loss of energy or tiredness, sometimes isolation, not wanting to socialize with others, not wanting to exercise; the very things that help people feel better are often things that they don't want to do.

Someone who is otherwise extroverted may go inside themselves, feel safe only at home, and become less concerned with their appearance or maintaining an adequately healthy diet, forgo doctor and dentist appointments when needed, and drink too much to subdue sad feelings and/or overuse medication.

As widows and widowers we may feel the world is empty, but realize that our sense of emptiness is temporary. Depression may be the dominant feature of your grief and may occur immediately after your loss, manifest itself gradually, or even surface after seeming recovery. That is part of the back and forth emotional roller coaster of grief.

It is not uncommon that as you are making progress, you regress, make progress, and then, regress again. Moving ahead and moving backward is a normal occurrence. You might even feel that you are doing too well, as if expecting the other shoe to drop. Or, if you do too well at first and then experience regression, that your healing has been lost. Actually, the anxiety over your loss often creates a surge of energy to run, to avoid; to participate in too many things; and when you finally slow down, some repressed feelings may return and with these feelings there is a sadness and depression. The frantic "running around" is an attempt to avoid *facing aloneness*.

Eighteen months after her husband passed away, Sue says, "I miss my husband so much, his companionship and everything that went along with that. I lost the love of my life, my best friend and my lover ... it has been devastating losing that package. I miss Peter as an individual. He was kind and caring and generous. I miss everything that he was."

Sue's coping strategy includes staying "busy, intellectually, mentally and physically." She is no longer teaching full time, but is tutoring and doing other volunteer work, "both feel good to me. I can focus all of my attention when I am doing this volunteer work.

"I would describe the phase I'm in now as 'coping'; I'm coming out of denial into depression. I'm taking medication for depression and it seems to be helping." Sue has been taking a low dose for about two months. "This has been just enough to minimize side effects of the medication and to help relieve the depression. The medication makes me feel lethargic and it affects the muscle coordination of my eyes. However, the medication has made it easier to cope with stress.

"I think I will be in this place for awhile. At times I feel like I'm on a pendulum that swings between denial and accepting the loss. To all appearances, I behave in the world differently than how I feel. My friends would say that I am doing well – taking care of the house, the yard and my financial difficulties. I would say I am coping well with the mechanical details of my life. However, I cover up my emotions except during my bereavement support group time once a week. I hope that, at some point, I will be able to move further away from the pain."

Paul has been gone for eighteen months, but for Sue the pain "is just as intense as during the early grieving. I feel very lucky that one of the legacies I will always cherish from my husband is 'optimism' and that helps me."

If you are feeling hopeless, you need the help of others to lead you out of your dilemma. You need an outreach approach, such as a bereavement support group, and this decision cannot be based solely on your ability to ask for help outright, since hopelessness itself may make it impossible for you to do so.

Despite loss, life does go on. However, you may be overwhelmed by feelings of helplessness set off by your loss. Seek help in identifying and expressing your feelings of anger, yearning, envy, hatred, and dependency. Helplessness and dependency can be softened by looking to solve problems, perhaps with help, but through your own efforts.

Sometimes we are unable, or unwilling, to experience anger directly. In many cases depression is anger turned inward instead of being directed to the real source. Many people are more comfortable being depressed than being angry. The best way to cope with these feelings is to speak them aloud, to get them into the open where they can be dealt with and resolved, rather than allowing them to smolder inside. During mourning we often try to deny our ambivalent feelings by idealizing our late spouse (i.e., not allowing feelings of anger toward our loved ones for leaving us, to surface).

Anxiety or fearfulness that persists may be a sign of uncompleted grief. We also have to factor in the amount of anxiety a person may have experienced even before the loss. General tenseness, difficulty in concentrating, sweatiness without a physical reason, flushing, and heart palpitations are symptoms of anxiety. You might even be unaware of the connection between your fears, unresolved grief, and ongoing anxiety.

Because grief can become internalized and turned into a physical illness, disease then acts as a substitute for unresolved sorrow. The loss of a loved one, if not successfully grieved and resolved, can precipitate a serious, even life threatening, illness. Depression can also be linked to a lower resistance to infection, and perhaps even reduce your immune defense capability.

Sometimes our grief is unfinished because our methods are not effective. For example, ruminating-about and being-obsessed-with sorrow are normal occurrences in the beginning of mourning, but they are ineffective tools months after death occurs. Often our grief is unfinished because we have found no comfortable way to release the complicated and mixed feelings we may have had about the deceased.

Few survivors escape without some feeling of guilt. People sometimes feel guilty because they did not make sure their spouse took care of his or her health, or saw the doctor sooner. Or, that their spouse died alone, for example, when they left the hospital room briefly, or were away from home. Yet, commonly it seems that we prefer to die alone, as reported time after time by the surviving spouse. Sometimes grief occurs over permission for a surgery and the patient doesn't recuperate; or they must arrange for their loved one to be taken off life support systems. A long illness may have led to resentment, and consequently guilt over that resentment. A sudden or accidental death may give rise to the torture of "if only's." Feeling guilty only adds to your negative view of yourself.

Given the information you may have now, you might have handled events differently. The reality is that you did the best you could at the time, and yet you may still feel guilty. Talk about it until you can let it go. Mourners are often tortured by regrets, repeatedly re-thinking real or imagined mistakes in the relationship with their loved one.

Guilt can also come from something we did or said that we wish that we had not done; or from something we think we should have said or done that we didn't do. Whenever you find yourself saying "Should," you are putting yourself in a position to feel guilt. You may even be creating guilt unreasonably. When you're thinking, "If only I hadn't bought the car," or "If only I hadn't left the hospital room or house," you are creating guilt by your self-talk. "If only" and "What if" are questions that can never be answered. You simply did not have the facts available at that time to know what else could have happened.

Feeling guilty may slow down your recovery. Even if you're convinced that your actions were wrong or insensitive, you must forgive yourself and go on with your life. Feeling guilty over a prolonged time is a choice you are making. But you can also choose not to feel guilty, by changing how you think about it. Guilt can lead to feelings of unworthiness, a desire to atone, self-punishment, and rejection of help from others. Guilt and anger can combine to cause a spiral of increasing isolation. Guilt can be one of the greatest obstacles to overcoming grief. It can arise from a number of sources and can be conscious or unconscious, recognized or well defended against.

Helpful Do's and Don'ts

Helpful Do's and Don'ts for the Bereaved

Do give yourself permission to not hurry your bereavement; it takes as long as it takes.

Do allow yourself to have a good time. You are entitled.

Do the rituals of purging the house when you feel up to the task.

Do take off the rings, when it feels like the right thing to do.

Do send out the thank you notes, when you feel ready to do this.

Do go out with your friends and socialize.

Do enjoy your life; you are entitled to do this.

Do develop single friends.

Do not worry about whether you are in the right place emotionally; you are exactly where you ought to be.

Do remember there are no "shoulds" in bereavement.

Helpful Do's and Don'ts
for Friends and Family of the Bereaved

Do stay supportive of where the bereaved is emotionally.

Do restrain yourself about offering unwanted and undesired opinions.

Don't tell your friends to give away the clothes until they are ready to do so.

Don't offer advice if you have not walked in their shoes.

Don't try to talk the bereaved into some other emotional place; be respectful of the emotional place they are in.

Don't be judgmental and critical.

Don't say, "Isn't that a big house for you to be in by yourself"?

Don't say, "Why don't you move to a smaller place?"

Do recognize that the bereaved might be very comfortable in their home and want to stay there.

Don't give "advice" unless you are asked.

Don't make harsh judgments if you have no feeling for what the bereaved is going though.

Please turn to page 301
for the Workbook section on this Time Sequence.

6.

Time Sequences of Healing Grief
Months Eighteen through Twenty-Four Months
Integration, Adjustment, Transition

While this feeling slowly snuck up on me, I began to realize that I am no longer seeing the world through my loss, although I still think of Rick daily. But a new challenge has come up. One in which I have found that moving from intellectual concept to emotional reality requires a giant leap of faith -- becoming involved in a new relationship. Is it possible to overlap loving someone new while still, to some degree, grieving for my late husband?

I am scared. After a half dozen blind dates, and no desire to see any a second time (I went on each because I felt that "it was time," and something I needed to do), I am dating someone, a widower whom I briefly met about six months ago. Being a widower himself, it took him this long to actually ask me out to dinner. When we first met, I had a feeling that he would eventually call, of course, I had no idea when. Not ready to date at that time, I put the feeling aside. He eventually called, we went out to dinner, and we've been a "we" ever since. And have I been fooling myself.

Almost two years into my mourning I <u>was</u> doing great: a satisfying career, good and loving friends and family around me, a satisfying balance in my life. I was feeling good, strong and grateful for the joy that my life once again embraced. And then "he" came along. I had moved beyond thinking that sex would again be part of my life, and that was fine, as I was putting my creative energies into other aspects of my life. While the idea of perhaps loving someone was always a possibility, intellectually I knew that if it happened, okay, if not, my life was fully satisfying.

Well, this new relationship has knocked me for the proverbial loop. I feel like a clueless teenager all over again. I am attracted to this man, emotionally, intellectually, and yes, physically. Naturally, he wants our relationship to become physically intimate; I want a level of emotional comfort. And I know that once our relationship becomes intimate, my feelings for him could very well change and I might no longer be a self-sufficient "I" but a "we" again. And that brings up so many difficult feelings. From the worry over his possible lack of attraction to my older body (I know that I still look good, but will he think so?). Do I want to see him naked? Am I able or even willing to give up the emotional comfort that I've worked so hard to obtain since my husband died? But then I tell myself, Sex is no big thing … it's only a physical act, pleasurable, but no big deal. WRONG!

Emotionally it is a big deal and I'm not sure he can understand these feelings since men are wired so differently in this area. And I still miss my husband. Is it even possible to overlap my loving and my grieving? What am I waiting for that will make it feel okay, a promise from him of a wonderful ever after? No, that would be a fool's promise that can't be made. My thoughts are vacillating between … Well, he just wants sex because he's a man and it's no big deal, I won't lose control over the life I've created or the ability to make it satisfying … to Oh, my, god, what if I fall in love with him? which, at 6:53 in the morning after a sleepless night, is a terrifying thought. And how would I tell my children? When are we a "couple?" How do I tell my stepchildren while reassuring them that this new love does not diminish the love I feel for their father, nor will it diminish the loving relationships we've carved out. I am also finding that he wants more of my time, while I'm still struggling to keep my safe life intact.

We went away for the weekend. Not "our" bed or "their" bed; but a lovely hotel room by the sea. We walked into the room, sat down at the table, each stuck in our own emotional space. I looked at him, he looked at me. "Does this feel as weird to you as it does me," I blurted out. YES! That helped. We talked. With our late spouses, we had each, after years of marriage, reached a level not only of intimacy, but perhaps even more important, ease at being together. Did we expect now to simply jump magically to that same level of comfort with each other? Probably. Unrealistic? Absolutely. We talked about it, and of our hidden expectations, some of which were unknown, even to ourselves. Once it was out in the open, we felt much more comfortable. Yes, perhaps we would EVENTUALLY become comfortable with each other knowing it would take time and that it was okay to feel awkward for now. Hard, but okay. This is so tiring; I need a nap.

Slowly I am beginning to trust this man. Or, perhaps, better said, I'm beginning to trust myself again to be emotionally safe and so, I am able to meet him halfway. It's still scary, but my level of comfort is growing. But I still struggle with the thought of feeling and showing affection for him with that emotional elephant in the room – my late husband. The reality is that this relationship has four people, two of which have a vote. It's sometimes crowded, sometimes distracting.

He is a widower with loving memories of his late wife. And that is good. But is he looking to my healing to heal him. Am I healed? Or, do I still need to hold my mourning pain dear? It is, after all, a safety net of sorts. Would I rather be an emotionally pampered widow, or a vulnerable newcomer to love? There is status in being the brave, resourceful widow who looked pain and loss in the eye and exclaimed, SO WHAT! But if he becomes emotionally dependent on me, will I feel treasured or suffocated? At this stage of life, it is so much easier, and harder, than dating and forming new relationships had been in our youth.

Common Questions

Why am I still having 'bad times' after being widowed for eighteen months?

Why did I think after two years I would feel better?

I do feel better, but some days I slip back, is that OK?

Why did some of my married friends go away?

Do I remind them of their own vulnerability and their own mortality?

I feel resentful sometimes that my married friends have each other and I don't have my partner. Is that normal?

How do I get out of myself and seek the larger world?

How do I find things to interest me when I get bored?

How do I get out of my own stuck places?

How do I encourage myself to go forward?

AT THIS POINT, you have generally worked through most of the grief issues of the last year and a half, or so. You are hopeful and involved in work or social activities, although you might still experience sadness and loneliness around special events (anniversaries, birthdays, and holidays). There are exceptions, however, and you may feel stuck at an earlier phase of grief.

New Romance

"First and foremost I will always love and be in love with my wife and the memory of my wife," says Hal. "Nothing and no one will ever change that. Gloria, my new partner, my friend, my lover, feels the same way about her late husband." Despite that, Hal admits that initially, he had quite a bit of guilt, feeling that he was betraying the memory of his wife in having another relationship.

"I'm Jewish, and that's one of the fundamentals of surviving after you've suffered the loss of a family member or spouse: It's that life must go on. And I believe in it. I believe that that's the way we are intended to heal." Now he has overcome his guilt feelings, believing that his late wife would want him to have a whole life and not a partial life. "I think that to have a whole life, a complete life, it's important to have someone to love besides your children, grandchildren and friends, but someone to be romantically in love with."

According to Laura, her new relationship with Sam was fraught with potential for being ambushed on all sides. "We had sensitivities because of my kids and my late husband's family whose members are very close. We really had to tread carefully. Actually we got 'outed' earlier on than we had wanted," says Laura.

"During the early stages of our becoming romantic we had taken to sitting out on the patio and sharing a glass of wine. One evening there was a little neck rubbing and a little kissing and a little 'kanoodeling' and that was very sweet until we were discovered by my 14-year-old son, who caught us in the act." Laura and Sam didn't want to pretend that nothing had happened because it would have been too dishonest. "So I acknowledged to my son that we were way more than friends. He said that, not only was he surprised, but very disturbed." Laura sympathized with the way he felt, realizing things were coming at him too fast. "It was too soon for him," Laura said, "because none of us had really processed his father's death, let alone grown comfortable with the idea that there was now a new man in the picture. Thankfully my younger son didn't act out, he just talked to me. He's an amazing kid.

"He was tearful when I told him that Sam and I were getting married." Her son was still grieving, and it was another change for him to deal with. He also had mixed feelings about Sam's coming to live in the house that his dad had built. "Yet he didn't act out against Sam," says Laura. "And I think that really showed his ability to be sensitive and to adapt to our new lives."

She is also grateful to Sam for his sensitivity. "To his credit, Sam's relationship with my son didn't include any kind of deception, nor did Sam try to be an authority figure." Although they talked to a professional counselor, they really hadn't known what to expect. "I even felt a little bad about maybe taking advantage of the fact that my son is a really good, deeply friendly kid who values our mother-son relationship and would go to great lengths not to harm it. He's not the kind of kid to lash out when he gets hurt."

With her older son, it was a different story. "He and I argued; he was more direct and angry. And he was more challenging. I ended up writing him a lengthy letter." The purpose of the letter was not to deny anything that he'd said, not to convince him of anything, or try to talk him into coming around. "I wrote it just to say, 'Here's how it is for me. I know that you had an incalculable loss and that a father is irreplaceable. I would never try to compare our losses because we're at different places in our lives, but here's what I'm faced with in deciding to make this commitment with Sam.'"

And then she described the advantage her son had had in growing up in a home with two committed adults who were dedicated to his welfare. "While your younger brother will never get his father back," she explained, "by my marrying Sam, he will have two committed adults supporting him and seeing to it that his life continues in its forward path.

"I didn't want to just live together with Sam, not because I have a moral problem with it, but because I didn't want things to stay up in the air, to be negotiable when they weren't." She believed a commitment was better than a half-step, and thought it would be better for her late husband's family too. "This wasn't a casual boyfriend, this was the real deal. And once we announced that we were getting married, it was time for everybody to put their opinions to rest. And they were magnificent. Even at our wedding, my late husband's mother stood up and gave this incredibly eloquent, toast; it was quite wonderful." They have done a remarkable job of embracing Sam, even though it is not always easy, Laura said. "They've been wonderful considering that in their tradition they mourn for a long time before even considering getting married again. They're amazing and very devoted to my kids."

One of the hardest things to accept was causing pain for people she loves dearly. "I really did choose to do what I needed to do," she acknowledges, "and that's hard. It was hard for my kids; it was too soon for my kids. But I don't know if it would have made any difference if I'd waited."

Laura's sons have since moved beyond initial dismay and have forged good relationships with Sam. "It is a credit not only to them and to Sam, but to my late husband as well. He was terrific in always letting the boys know how much he loved them and how important they were to him. It made his loss very painful for them, but also helped them in their healing, I think. They didn't have a lot of unresolved stuff to settle with him; they were very secure in their relationship with their dad." Laura's advice to somebody who is mourning the loss of their partner/spouse is to try to accept those first moments when you begin to feel a little okay, and not freak out about it. "Try not to feel bad about that," she said. Instead, try to realize that unhappiness is something you have to move through, not a state you have to maintain forever as a testament to your lost spouse. And even while the pain is still there, don't resist when life hands you an opportunity to live again, to experience love or pleasure in whatever capacity or dimension." Don't fight it, she said. "Allow yourself to release some of that pain, knowing that your late spouse will stay in your heart; you're just releasing grief and releasing grief is not the same as forgetting ... you won't do that."

Are you ready to start a relationship? Some will say "yes" because they are lonely, while others will have healed sufficiently to want to share their lives by coming together out of strength rather than simply need. You might feel scared of forming a new relationship because you feel out of "practice," or fear rejection, and may not feel capable of altering your dating outlook to fit into today's changed social system. Feelings of betrayal and guilt are also commonly felt, and you may be reluctant because grown children or friends might object and be prone to compare your new partner or date, to your late spouse.

It is a tribute to human nature that we have the willingness and patience to see if we can come together with a new partner and grow in spite of our differences. We do have the ability to bring to each new relationship a uniqueness that needs to be valued. With that in mind, are you willing to try again, to deepen a possible new friendship and give it a chance to grow?

Can people truly fall "in love" earlier in their bereavement? There are several concerns for those who try. In reality you can't be available to love someone else until you have healed *enough*. Nor can you be available emotionally to someone else until you are emotionally available to yourself in a healthy way.

Some widows and widowers form a new relationship too early, out of loneliness and fear they would not make it alone. While it is not uncommon for people to began dating at around the fifth month of mourning, if you have not healed enough in your mourning before taking on a new relationship, the unfinished business sometimes comes back later. Yet, if the mourning period and the new love overlap, both can co-exist if sufficient mourning and healing have taken place. After the first year, with sufficient experience in healing, there is more ego strength to build a new relationship.

In thinking about new relationships, invariably what come up are possessions. For example: in taking on a new relationship, you might wonder how to blend what you own with what your new partner has. "If I move into his house, what do I do with what I have?" Deleting, discarding, sorting and throwing out become tasks of utmost importance and pain; associations resurface and memories of events associated with certain objects flood back. Metaphorically, the "house" represents the self. The need to hold onto things represents holding onto the old life. Therefore, appropriate exploration is necessary in order to gain a deeper understanding of the symbolism and the meaning of possessions. In new relationships, one has to be able to give up some of the past in order to emerge beyond it and live in the "now."

Old Friends Lost

"My married friends of many years have abandoned me." You might be feeling that many of your old friends now find you a threat, don't know how to relate or talk to you, or feel awkward around you, and visa-versa. Old friends may identify with the deceased spouse, and their own mortality causes them to retreat. Widows especially often feel like a "fifth wheel" in a group when issues such as, who pays for dinner or the theatre arise, causing one to be uncomfortable. It helps to arrange ahead of time to take care of money issues, or pay back friends by inviting them out to dinner or to your home. Or, perhaps you have coped with this feeling of abandonment by making new single/widowed friends either from your bereavement support group or some other place. Perhaps you initiated dropping out of your married friends' lives because it was too painful and there were too many memories.

Lingering Feelings

"Why am I still having 'bad times' after being widowed for eighteen months? For some, the second year can be worse because denial has worn off, and the reality of being alone has set in. Friends and relatives assume you are better and leave you alone, although you still may find that the responsibilities of your life, working or making decisions alone, depressing.

Or, "I am beginning to feel better and I feel guilty." This guilt has to do with feelings of betrayal toward your late spouse. This feeling is normal. It is helpful to look at what you are specifically feeling guilty about. Is it realistic and what can be done? Or is it unrealistic, and how can you make some peace with it? Be aware that feeling guilty at feeling better interferes with your healing and that it may be necessary to look at the reasons why you may not want to heal.

Leaving Your Bereavement Support Group

"I'm going to be coming to the end of the two years and know that it is time to leave my bereavement support group." Talk about this feeling way before the time to leave. This separation occurs on two levels: physical and emotional. Talking starts the emotional separation. It is important at this point to actively find other activities where you can get the friendship and support that your group now provides. Consider taking classes, attend lectures or workshops or get together with friends during the time you normally met with your bereavement support group. Reflect on your current feelings and the progress you have made over the last two years or so.

"Dear Friends," wrote Hal to his bereavement support group. "When I entered this bereavement support program 'kicking and screaming' most of you saw me at the lowest point in my life. As the months rolled on you saw a change in me as I saw change in all of you. We, in our 'darkest hour,' clung to each other and through our tears and unbearable grief started a healing process orchestrated and fostered by our support group and facilitators. Now after all of the countless group sessions, dinners and get-togethers we have started to move on and have created a new type of life for ourselves ... not the one we had hoped to have with our beloved mates, but a different kind of life that fate has given us."

Hal adds that although they aren't completely healed, and may never be the same as they were before, they have all learned a great deal from the group and each other. "We now can proceed knowing that most of the trauma we experienced was experienced by us all and that we are not 'crazy.'"

In other circumstances, it's doubtful that any in the group would have met. "But that wonderful and somewhat strange thing called 'group' happened, and here we are closer to each other than we would ever have imagined ... and that is so good and so healing. While our old friends are still there we have a sad and unique bond that makes our friendship very special and meaningful."

Hal explained that his healing has progressed to the point that he has decided to discontinue participation in the Bereavement Support Group. "I am happy that soon all of you will be 'graduating' from our support group while continuing with our social get-togethers. I send my love and gratitude to you all. -- Hal"

If possible, this is a good time to help others who are in the beginning of their mourning and healing process. You've been there and are sensitive to their concerns about "Will life get better? Will I heal?" By being helpful to others, by answering their questions positively, you can also gauge your own growth and healing.

You finally understand the difference between "aloneness" and "loneliness." You can acknowledge that one can feel alone in a crowd but that loneliness is a different concept. You are also ready now to acknowledge the contribution of laughter; the response to joy, the need to laugh to offset the heaviness that accompanies mourning. It is becoming easier to laugh and enjoy again, understanding that humor greatly contributes to healing.

Integration, Adjustment and Transition

How will you know when you are healing? When you can think of your loved one without the accompanying strong emotion of longing and sadness. When you are healing, you will remember him or her more realistically, neither as an idealized saint nor a villain. You will be living in the present, not stuck in the past, and making plans for the future. You will notice that the deceased is in your thoughts less and less as you actively build a continuing life. Joys and pleasures may be experienced again, alone or with others.

Mourning is a process that, simply put, takes as long as it takes. Bill's wife died eighteen months ago, and at first, the only emotion he felt was anger. Anger directed at the doctor who took care of his late wife. "The doctor delayed, for almost four months, tests that would have diagnosed my wife's illness. Had they been run, an earlier diagnosis would probably not have saved her life, but it would most certainly have helped make her more comfortable." After finally running the test, the doctor came to Bill in the waiting room and said, "I'm embarrassed, but I have some bad news for you."

"And I was pissed!"

Bill says he didn't find himself in denial at any time in his bereavement because he was with his wife as her disease progressed until she passed away. "I was very emotional over her death," he said. "There was no way I could bottle up the pain I felt, or deny that my wife was gone." Yet, while his wife was ill, he wouldn't let her see his tears. "I would go outside to cry. I thought to myself, How could such a lovely person suffer so much?"

The first week after his wife died, Bill was numb, so mentally and physically exhausted that he couldn't even cry. "I think I got all that out of the way before she died." After several weeks he joined a bereavement support group and now says, "Oh-my-god, I don't know how I would have gotten through that time without them."

Looking back, Bill can say he doesn't feel anger over lost opportunities, because he and his wife had a full life, traveling and doing mainly what they wanted to do. "I wish we could have had more years together, but the reality is that we had more enjoyment together than most people have in a whole lifetime."

After about eighteen months, Bill started dating again. "It is an experience! I feel like a teenager again." And even though he is older and perhaps wiser, he still goes through the fear of being rejected. He worries whether the woman will like him, worries whether he'll like her, but has concluded he is usually happier dating a widow rather than a divorcee. "Widows are better because we can relate to each other more. A divorcee seems to have an 'agenda' or anger from their former marriage. It's nicer to be with someone who has beautiful memories of their spouse." Widows seem better able to understand his need to embrace the memory of his late wife, Bill said, and in this way, bring her into the relationship, just as widows do, in remembering their late husband.

Bill is currently dating several women, and is attracted to more than one. Will he marry again? "If it happens, it happens, but it's not a goal of mine," he says. "My goal at this point is to have fun. If I was to get into a serious relationship that would be fine, but I'm not thinking 'ahead of the game.'"

When he first started dating, Bill felt disloyal to his late wife, which is a common experience. "I will never forget my late spouse or my love for her, but I know in my heart that she would want me to go on." He has also learned the futility of comparing the women he is dating to her. "I've come to understand that while no one will replace her, I can look forward to having some wonderful times." When he started dating, Bill noticed that his adult children, especially his daughter, started to parent him, wanting to meet every woman he went out with, and asking whether he would ever marry again. "I had to remind my daughter that I'm still her father and when I'm serious about somebody, she will meet her. When I don't agree with my daughter, she says I'm not listening. My answer? I'll always 'listen' to you, but I won't always agree with you and that's my right." Bill and his daughter have always been close, but when she tried to take over parenting, he felt he had to put his foot down. Yet, he is concerned. "I don't want my daughter and somebody I get serious with to be enemies. That would destroy me."

Now Bill is at the point of integrating his old life while creating a satisfying new life. Holidays are still difficult and will probably continue to be, but are becoming easier. "While a year ago I was really unhappy, today when these things come up it doesn't destroy me."

He looks back almost in amazement at how far he has come in a year. "If you had told me a year ago that I would be laughing and cracking jokes, I would have said that's impossible. I was absolutely wrong. It is hard for people new to mourning to believe, but it does happen. I certainly thought it impossible that I would ever want to date again."

Yet here he is, amazed at feeling so good, and enjoying being with people again. "I have come such a long way, it is truly unbelievable."

You will know you are healing when you can think of your loved one without the strong emotional feelings of longing and sadness. Sometimes it is helpful to complete the unfinished business of the relationship by writing a letter to your late spouse. In this way you can finish old thoughts or conversations that are otherwise carried on in your head. Writing a letter to say goodbye is also helpful - a way to express feelings about being left. The release of these feelings is a cathartic process.

You are healing when you begin to remember him/her more realistically. You will be living in the present, not stuck in the past, and making plans for the future. Coming to peace with the lost loved one does not erase the love or the memories. It does mean that you have accepted the death, that the pain and sorrow have lessened, and that you feel free to reinvest in your life. Your late spouse will be in your thoughts less and less. You will be living in the present, not stuck in the past, and making plans for the future. You will let go of the intense pain, rather than the memories.

In December of 1999, Nancy's husband Charles was diagnosed with Lou Gehrig's disease. "The doctor handed me a brochure explaining the disease," said Nancy "and suggested I call the ALS Association. I knew there was nothing we could do except to try to prolong his life and make every day as good as possible."

Charles was a Real Estate Developer in the middle of a big project that he had been working on for ten years. Once he became ill, Nancy worked in the office with him, trying to get a grasp of the immensity of the project. "Despite the loss of speech and his weakening condition, he continued to go into the office until February of 2002. He died the following April."

Nancy and Charles had been married for 32 years and "not a day went by without him saying 'I love you.' He loved to dance, to laugh and to make people laugh. He thoroughly enjoyed life. He also loved his work, despite any difficulty. He would look on adversity as a challenge and showed incredible strength under pressure. Charles' cup was always overflowing; plus he was blessed with a great sense of dignity and integrity. He had an unusually quick wit and when asked what sustained our marriage would answer, 'A sense of humor.' He made everything better; he refused to see the darkness.

"This very refusal is what left me with financial and familial problems when he passed away. His son and daughter-in-law had conspired to take over the business, even before Charles died. I learned this when, after my husband's death, I asked his son for his tax attorney's number, needing a tax attorney at that time." When Nancy called the attorney, he said that he couldn't represent her because there was a conflict. "That was the first I learned about their intentions."

This was a shock. Nancy had raised Charles' son from the age of 13, along with his sister and her own two teenagers. She thought they had been one happy family with three grandchildren whose births, birthday parties and holidays celebrations she attended. "My step-children called me 'Mom' and our combined children (from previous marriages) referred to each other as brother and sister. I thought of Charles' children as my own," says Nancy. "Now I had to face a lawsuit brought on by his son.

"I'm told that people change and families break up over money. I never knew it could be so vicious. I finally settled with them at the end of 2003 and held on to the business. I had to finish the project myself which included working with the city, resolving two other lawsuits, and paying old debts and loans that Charles had accumulated; all this while mourning his death."

Has Nancy felt put-upon through all this? Has she been angry with Charles? "Yes, I have, but I haven't regretted one moment of the life I had with Charles. I miss the grandchildren; perhaps one day they will show up at my door. Taking care of Charles during his illness was a privilege, but yes, I have been angry with Charles, at times, since his passing. But those times didn't last long. I could never stay angry for long because I loved him absolutely."

Charles has been gone now for almost three years. For Nancy, the grieving and healing was a slow process. "The first thing I did was to engage a therapist. Next I joined a bereavement support group where I met wonderful friends who understood the roller coaster of emotions during mourning. We shared and continue to share times of longing; we understand each other because we are all experiencing varying degrees of the same emotions.

"At my bereavement support group I met a very caring and thoughtful man who lost his wife after 53 years of marriage. We both know that no one can replace the one we lost, in fact we both have times of missing our spouses even when we are together." Yet, Nancy has gone on to create a fulfilling new life. "I know that Charles would want me to be happy even though he knew I would miss his touch," Nancy adds with a chuckle.

For integration, adjustment and transition to take place, you must learn to rebuild your life and learn how to integrate your loss. All of this is a slow process: accepting the reality of the loss and returning to physical and psychological well-being. There will be less crying, less intensity of tears, and restoration of self-esteem, as you focus on the present and future. You will begin to develop the capacity to enjoy life again. And you will even derive pleasure from the awareness of your own growth.

Discovering who you are, as an "I" rather than a "we," is hard work and a major task of bereavement. Visualize if you will two overlapping circles which represent the relationship. After loss, the major task is to find out who you are without your spouse; when you have been married for many years that can feel overwhelming.

Ideally, when we love someone who has died, we must thoroughly experience all the feelings evoked by our loss as we gradually say goodbye to our loved one and resume our lives. To recover fully from a loss means to complete the tasks of mourning and to slowly let go of the pain. Completing our mourning does not erase the love or the memories, but it does mean that we are moving towards accepting the death; the sorrow has lessened and we feel free to reinvest in our lives.

Helpful Do's and Don'ts

Helpful Do's and Don'ts for the Bereaved

Do attend social events if you wish to. Do listen to your intuition, but don't attend events because of pressure from friends.

Do take your own car, so you can leave when you wish.

Do be aware that although a religious ceremony might mark the end of mourning, you might feel differently. Do allow yourself to feel the way you do, noting that your feelings are subject to change.

Don't accept the well-meaning advice of friends. It might make you angry, even though they are well intentioned, because they have not been bereaved and don't know how you feel.

Do know that as time goes on, you might feel worse.

Do know that as time passes, your emotions become more exposed and raw. Do know that early feelings are masked by shock and denial and that as feelings emerge, you may feel more depressed than before, and that this is normal.

Do not wait for the phone to ring, reach out and call a friend if you are feeling low.

Do know that it is OK to want to date.

Do know that dating can cause two conflicting thoughts: This is okay and I want to do it, <u>and</u>, I feel disloyal to my spouse.

Don't sit home feeling sorry for yourself.

Do get out, reach out and find single friends.

Do know that it is normal to be with your married friends and feel like a third wheel.

Do get out into the sunshine and weed the garden.

Do make flower arrangements on days when you hardly feel like it.

Do change the water in the vases, snip back and talk to the flowers. Encourage them to open.

Don't pull the blinds during the day. Let fresh air in and get the breeze.

Do enjoy the sunshine.

Do walk in the rain.

Do participate in life and be grateful.

Do determine that you are entitled to feel joy again.

Do stay connected with the people you have met in your support group. Leaving the security of the group may leave a void on group night. Many people stay connected and continue to see each other and socialize for years. There is a great comfort in keeping the new friends you have made through this difficult experience.

Do not compare the current dating partner with your spouse. This may seem inevitable, but each person is unique in his own way. Be open to a new experience, new love, new pleasure, recognizing it will not be the way it was ... in some ways it might be better and surely it will be different.

Helpful Do's and Don'ts for Friends and Family
of the Bereaved

Do give the bereaved enough room to discover for themselves what is really going on at this point.

Don't try to take the mourner's problems away from them; allow them to deal with their problems in their own way.

Do not offer religious solace when you sense they are not ready for it. It might be your value, not theirs.

Don'ttalk about your experience, making theirs seem unimportant.

Do not refuse their thanks by saying, "I really haven't done anything."

Do not cut them off before they finish speaking or finish their sentence for them.

Do not have an answer for their problem before they're finished telling you what their problem is.

Do give them enough room to discover for themselves what is really going on.

All of the above equal having respect for the mourner's intelligence and their ability to know what is best for themselves.

Moving Beyond

It is time to welcome your "self" back to the world of the living and participate fully in it. There is only the moment of now, not to be missed – to be present in the world and present with yourself. In this way you will be alive and awakened again. In despair you were closed off, empty and drained. In happiness you can feel fully, be giving and loving and less self-centered. In full participation, you can rejoice in your life and make it active and fun.

You have made a conscious choice to participate fully in life once again and with your eyes wide open – a conscious choice to hear the symphony instead of never again buying a ticket. You are able once again to invite the experience of living and choose among difficult choices. There is a new place you have entered because you are ready to transcend and heal, and it calls up your hidden talents and expressions. It calls up the creative energy you have within and want to express, even when you don't think that you have it

You are completing your journey of integration, adjustment and transition, your journey through loss, to life and laughter. Bravo!

Please turn to page 322
for the Workbook section on this Time Sequence.

Healing through Creating Balance
Jo Christner, Psy.D.

The death of your spouse most likely turned your whole world upside down ... out of balance. Everything seemed to change in your life ... especially you. Your belief system, physical routines such as sleep, energy and eating, emotional stability, relationships ... even your environment has taken on a different meaning. That feeling of safety, comfort and familiarity about your life no longer seems to exist.

Grieving is a difficult journey, as you already know. In the process you and your life will change. Learning to re-create a sense of *balance* is essential. Balance assists the healing process and maintains emotional, spiritual and physical health and stability.

An architect needs a blueprint to build a new masterpiece. A ship's captain needs a compass and maps to reach his destination safely. As you build a new identity and life, you too can benefit from a *"blueprint"* or guide to creating balance in your life. I have created such a *"map,"* an acronym "**S.P.A.C.E.,**" which represents balance and stands for all the areas in which we spend time in our lives. If you learn to create balance around and within you, you can feel good about life again.

S: Spiritual – How do you spend time with your soul?
Maybe you are questioning your spirituality or religious beliefs and this may feel like a difficult area ... one of confusion, anger, emptiness and possibly representing another loss. "If there were a God, why would He allow this to happen?" As you walk through the grieving process, you can find answers in many ways.

- Seek professional help through therapy or religious counseling.
- Plan ways to ease your soul and find some peace ... sunsets, walks in nature, gardening; service to others, spending time with children; listen to nurturing music; practice meditation and deep breathing exercises.
- Prayer – sometimes it's nice to share your thoughts without getting advice and judgments.
- Begin a journal – write about one blessing that you have each day. Blessings are often *"small"* things that we take for granted, like our health, food and shelter. Everyone has blessings. You just need to acknowledge them.

P: Physical – how do you spend time with your body?
With your loss, your entire being may feel as though it has been traumatized. Physically, your strength and energy may have declined, leaving you feeling weak and exhausted. Along with depression and grieving, many of our physical habits are changed: SLEEP, you may

experience insomnia, many awakenings or not wanting to wake up or get out of bed; APPETITE, you may be eating very little or wanting to stuff down all those feelings by eating too much, causing a loss or gain in normal weight; and, ENERGY, you may feel like you have to drag yourself to do even the smallest task, or maybe you keep extremely busy so you won't have to feel.

This is the time to be aware of your body's needs and to nurture it back to health and balance. Nurture your body and the awareness and feelings will follow.

- Exercise. This is a well-documented way to lift depression and energy. Walking for 20 to 30 minutes three times a week is a great beginning. (If you have health problems, confer with your doctor.)
- Get outside. The natural Vitamin D from sunshine (in moderation) profoundly affects hormonal balance.
- Get a massage. Touch is often terribly missed after the loss of a spouse.
- Take a yoga class. Yoga poses improve blood circulation, which could improve your energy and dissipate feelings of lethargy.
- Deep breathing and meditation. Both help to lower anxiety and improve much needed sleep.
- Aromatherapy can alter brain chemistry right through your nose! Lavender, for example, induces restfulness for many.

A: Affect –How do you spend time with your feelings?
Affect is a psychological term for the range of ups and downs of your everyday feelings. You may feel as though you are no longer interested in pleasurable activities. That is normal. Do things to nurture and honor your feelings.

- Be around positive, supportive people. That's why bereavement support groups are so important.
- Honor your feelings—there is healing in tears. If you find that you "can't cry," know that it may be time or maybe your tears have already been shed. Don't judge them. Just let them be.
- Music can be a very healing therapy. Listen to music that you like. Slow and relaxing music can help you calm down and sleep better. It can also lift your spirits and let you sing.
- Seek professional help if you feel stuck or the pain is just too intense. It doesn't mean that you are weak or "crazy," rather in more pain than you can get through alone.
- Communicate with nature. Visit the mountains, seashore or sit in your garden. Nature has a way of healing and lifting your spirits.
- Give yourself permission to laugh. It doesn't take away from the grieving process. It honors the memory of your spouse and the life that you had together.

C: Cognitive – How do you spend your time with your thoughts?

Your thoughts are a very important part of the healing process that can either impede or support healthy grieving. Often, it is difficult to "turn off" your thoughts … fears about the future, memories about the past and anxious thoughts about what you will possibly do without your spouse by your side.

The way that we *think* affects the way that we *feel* which affects our *behavior* and the way that we *perceive* the world,(i.e., *"I'll always be alone now."* = feelings of sadness, hopelessness = a behavior of staying home alone = a perception that the world is a lonely place).

Be aware of your thoughts and begin to learn to "reprogram" them to support your healing process, (i.e., *"I feel lonely since my spouse died, but I'll get through this with the help of others."* = feelings of hope and support = the behavior of going to a bereavement support group = a perception that you are not alone in this world).

- Begin to use "affirmations" (positive statements about yourself) such as *"I am a strong, loving person who will survive."*
- Utilize a therapist to identify and change your thoughts.
- Write your thoughts in a journal. You'll begin to see patterns and have a place to express your feelings.
- Take a class such as art, music or history, to expand your thinking.

E: Environment – How do I spend time in my environment?

Think about your environment, such as pets, plants, light, music, garden, pictures, people, etc. The way that we mold our environment has an effect on the way that we feel and think. Create your environment to work for you in this healing process, not against you. If a sad song comes on the radio that causes you distress, it's okay to turn the knob to find a station that is uplifting.

- Clean up the clutter. If need be, have a friend or a professional organizer assist you. *"Clutter creates confusion."* Right now you have enough confusion in your life.
- If you like spending time outdoors in nature, remember to do that. Often we sit inside in front of the TV or staring out the window. Energy follows energy. You need to move your energy and eventually more energy will follow.
- Be with positive people that you enjoy and like.
- Go places that you enjoy and/or feel safe (i.e., art museums and theater, a favorite park, temple or church).
- Music can be positively distracting and nurturing.

Think about the five areas of **S.P.A.C.E.: Spiritual, Physical, Affect, Cognitive and Environment**. Write "S. P.A.C.E." vertically on a piece of paper and write your own ideas or activities in each of the five areas. This will become *your* "blueprint" to rebalancing your life. Plan to include something from each area of your life on a weekly basis. Eventually, one step at a time, one day at a time, *your* life will again begin to have balance and you will begin to heal.

The captain of a ship can't embark without
first knowing his destination.
Otherwise,
no matter if he has the most
sophisticated ship ever made,
he's going to end up lost.
Author Unknown

7.

Mourning Non-Traditional Relationships

THE PAIN OF grieving is there for all losses, whether spouse or lover. A partnership transcends labels and roles and one's partner is primary when a strong bond exists. Regardless of how the relationship is named, the pain of loss requires healing. In life, we may be exposed to mini losses several times before a major loss presents itself. We "deal with it" and even understand it to a small degree. Yet, we are not schooled in loss or prepared for it in life, so when we experience a larger loss it can feel devastating.

When we love and lose someone, whether that someone is lesbian, homosexual, bisexual or transgender, we are overwhelmed by pain and sorrow. However, when our relationship is out of the mainstream, we might already have been so criticized and saddened, that in this final loss, we find it much more difficult to grieve, heal and move on to a fulfilling new life.

No one can understand totally the pain of another. We can meet at waysides of commonality and share our experiences and progress, and although there is healing in the act of sharing, we still feel alone in our sadness. What touches us in a positive way is when we feel understood. The loneliness of loss and alienation affects us deeply at the level of our souls.

Mourning the loss of a partner within a non-traditional relationship can encompass an additional burden if there is little family or community-at-large support. Such relationships may have had less approval, or in the case of a gay, lesbian, bisexual or transgender partner, even have been kept secret. If the immediate family is not approving of this relationship, they have trouble being supportive. In fact, they may not understand, but may also be angry over the relationship. The reality is that out of the mainstream experiences are harder to understand and accept when they are not "your experience."

Parents who have accepted their non-mainstream children, who love and support them, don't have to understand everything. Their love is a support platform. That said, however, joining a traditional support group may not be seen as a viable option because there is no common ground. Parents who are grieving want to meet other parents who are grieving. Grown children who are grieving want a group with others like themselves. Widows/widowers prefer being with other widows/widowers although there are similarities, there are many differences. People want a good match, the compatibility that comes with shared understanding and similarities. People who are gay do not see a mainstream support group as a major support for themselves because "they will not understand." People want a match for their experience; they want to know that they can feel understood and loved and not judged or ridiculed. They will drop out of mainstream grief support groups that don't accept them.

When Doug's partner died in 1993, he didn't feel anger right away. "I was in shock and numb, with a feeling of painful loss. At first I didn't try to find a bereavement support group, but later, when I asked around in the area I lived in, Connecticut, I was told that a group for gay men was not available so I worked with an independent therapist for three or four years," says Doug.

After his partner's death, Doug was faced with taking on the responsibilities of their old life together, which his partner had done effortlessly. "This became extremely difficult. My lover left a large estate, well in excess of one million dollars. He had chosen his business partner as his executor and in the first year of probate it became very clear that the executor was not interested in protecting my interests in the will."

It took nine years to get the case heard in Superior Court. "Because my attorney didn't prepare for the trial, or investigate all the assets and cash that should have been there for me, the executor mismanaged turning over the property and cash to me which would have paid the estate taxes, although the blood family was immediately granted their cash bequests.

"The Superior Court finally found the executor at fault and the estate was to have been put back to where it should have been in 1996 had the estate been handled properly; to date, March of 2005, this still has not happened. Also, while my attorneys felt we had won, the money was hard to find because it was hidden. A fraction of it was received.

"My lover died of AIDS; I had been his full-time lover for 14 years. I took care of him for the last year which took a toll on my health; I was HIV positive since 1988. It was stressful knowing my lover was dying. When the lawyers saw me, I'm sure they felt I wouldn't live long enough to see the money anyway."

Doug is angry and depressed. "I'm on antidepressant meds as well as seeing a therapist weekly. Part of my problem, I feel, is that I have had no closure. My lover infected me with the disease. I am not finished with the estate. My partner wanted certain things done in a certain way, which I'm trying to do. Some of my friends are encouraging me to just let it go. But I'm a fighter.

"Unfortunately I have no family to support me emotionally. I did not come out to my parents that my partner was gay. They saw him as a business partner, roommate and friend. I'm from Oklahoma. My brothers, nieces, uncles knew but not my mother or father. My parents are bigoted, so I felt best to let it alone. When my partner died, my brother asked for my permission to tell my mother, which I gave. He told her I was gay and asked that she be supportive. Not only wasn't that something she could accept or do, but now we're all totally estranged — we don't talk at all.

"Although I thought that I had begun to heal over the first six years of mourning, I have not recovered from my loss because over the last five months I have been forced to continue to fight for his wishes to be carried out and this has thrown me back to when he first died. Yet, in a way, I have to keep him alive. His face and voice are always in my head. My therapist made a wonderful suggestion. She suggested I create a category in my brain for him and file it away. Thankfully it has helped, it has made a tremendous difference.

"Because I was so distracted by the estate battle, I believe that I only went though part of the grieving process. I cried everyday for the first two years. I was grieving for myself as well. He was my life partner and life changed without him. The most painful part of mourning was in my dreams. He would be smiling at me, but I was so hurt that he wasn't there when I woke. The first two years were the hardest.

"I felt isolated because at that time there weren't support groups available for gay men and I didn't know where to turn for support. I know that in San Francisco, for example, that there are limited community resources for grieving. I'm sure that a support group would have helped me. I still do. I really believe, at least in those years, that there was very limited help available in the way of support groups and I also think that people have a different, negative attitude when loss is related to AIDS."

While grieving and healing is never easy, note the positive difference when support is available.

Clark & Robert

Clark and Robert met when both were in graduate school on the East Coast. They started dating soon into their first year and were together for almost twelve years at the time of Robert's death. For the most part, both had wonderful family support for their relationship. However, there was one caveat, adds Clark. "My father, who died when Robert and I had been together about eight years, never wanted Robert to spend the night at their house when we would visit for holidays. His expression was "'I've accepted you, but I don't have to accept your friends.'" Clark has a number of siblings, who, upon hearing this, immediately offered their homes for family visits and distanced themselves from their father's attitude. It is interesting to note that though his family is quite religious, despite the teaching of their church, it is to their credit that Clark has always felt like a valued member of the family. They accepted Robert as an "in-law," and both were well respected by his siblings.

"My partner's father was more accepting than mine," says Clark. "We also had many supportive friends, and were open about our relationship in our graduate program. I have to say, I feel I was lucky." They were never harassed or negatively affected by being an openly gay couple in school or in our community, Clark said. He even got his first job through a recommendation by Robert's father.

About five years into their relationship, Robert tested positive for HIV. This was in the mid-1980s, and the life expectancy then was two-to-four years after testing positive. "Our grieving process began on the day when he got a positive test result. At a time when, ideally, we would have been entering careers for which we had worked so hard, Robert recognized that his life would likely be cut short. I anticipated that we would not fulfill our dreams together."

They adjusted, and it was roughly two years before Robert developed any symptoms. When symptoms did develop and he required medication, he had bad reactions to most of the medications available at that time. "His health was deteriorating fast. He went on disability, a huge blow to him, and a scary time in our relationship because we were a young, upwardly mobile couple, and now he was dealing with DSHS and social workers helping to insure his medical benefits."

Unfortunately, Robert was unable to live long enough to benefit from the newer, protease inhibiter medications. He had suffered several illnesses, but the worst thing was that he was becoming confused and losing his memory. "He had talked about not wanting to suffer and I, somewhat selfishly, asked him not to take his own life. I told him that I'd work with his doctors to prevent it," adds Clark. "He reluctantly agreed, but, six months later, as his condition worsened, without telling me, he decided to take his life.

"I left home early one Sunday morning to run a few errands, and when I phoned Robert, there was no answer. I found him dead in our bed; he had killed himself after all." His biggest mistake, Clark said, was in calling 911 because the paramedics tried to resuscitate Robert, who had already provided "Do Not Resuscitate" orders to the hospital. "In my confusion I wasn't thinking about that. It also was unnerving, because when someone commits suicide at home, the coroner and the police need to investigate. Not only was I devastated by his death, but I was being asked why certain knives were lying out on countertops, and so on. All in all, the police were exceptionally kind, but doing their job."

Because of Robert's illness, Clark had begun grieving prior to his death. Yet, as is often the case with a prolonged illness leading to death, Clark admits that he still was not prepared. "Given the circumstances it was shocking, says Clark. "I'd pictured him dying quietly in my arms in the hospital surrounded by family and friends, not my coming home on a damp winter day and seeing a dead body.

"Having gone through it, I am not convinced of the stage models of grieving. I don't think my grief was clear-cut in any progressive way. There was no denial or anger ... there was emotional freefall." Clark doesn't remember much about the first few months following Robert's death. He threw himself into work, and he started dating too soon. Initially, his relationships were usually based on physical attraction; he had a brief reawakening of sexual feelings that had been buried during Robert's long illness. It was, however, only a distraction.

"I believed at the time that I had grieved deeply and prepared before he died, and that now I was ready to move on, but that was not true." For over a year following Robert's death, Clark was mostly distracted with other relationships, work, and with remodeling their house. For nearly ten years after Robert died, he struggled to find the right relationship. "I'm now in a great relationship, for the right reasons, and I have a house that feels like a home for the first time since Robert died."

Clark recalled that in the first weeks following Robert's death, good friends were around often, which helped with the grieving process. "I don't think my grief was different, the support I got different, or the confusion and anguish I felt any different from anyone having just lost a spouse. There were no children, so in some ways it was easier than it would probably have been if I'd needed to comfort them as well."

In the early 1990s, gay men who lost partners to AIDS had a community of other gay men who had lost partners to AIDS. There were other friends dying at that time also, and for years after Robert's death "there were a series of memorial services for friends. I felt a close bond with the grieving partners and families."

Clark did not join an official support group, but wisely did enter individual therapy to help clear up confusion about his personal life. His family was supportive from afar. "I experienced, as many people do, the loss of some mutual friends who stopped coming to the house Robert and I had lived in because it 'held bad memories' or because 'I reminded them of Robert and it made them sad.' The first time this happened was the most shocking and the most intensely painful," Clark said, "but the hardest time came three or four months afterward. People had moved on, and were slightly exasperated with my grief process, a little less tolerant of my tearing up around them, and I began to spend more time with people who never knew Robert, or at home alone feeling blue."

Robert's family continued to be supportive, but when they talked, it seemed they only made each other sadder. "Thankfully, we've stayed in contact. I continue to have his siblings in my life and we don't feel that sadness any longer, but enjoy a mutual sharing of having been a part of Robert's life.

"There was not much about being in a 'non-traditional relationship' that impacted my grieving process. I work with, and exist among a lot of very sophisticated and supportive people. Everyone understood that I had lost my spouse, even if the relationship was not officially recognized. When one of my siblings lost a spouse several years after Robert died, my family called me to say 'They'll need to talk to you; you understand what it is like.'"

Clark says his pain was never seen as something different. He was acknowledged as Robert's partner in the hospital before he died, and had medical power of attorney, enabling him to make needed arrangements. "His family respected that, and I did not have any trouble such as one hears about when families swoop in and don't allow a gay partner to see their dying loved one. That was as far from my experience as one could get. I suspect, sadly, that there are those horrifying scenarios. I'm not sure that I even needed more documentation, other than a letter of testamentary, in order to pick up death certificates. I assume a married heterosexual spouse would need the same. For me, the only difference in my situation was that we were two men."

Helpful Do's and Don'ts

Helpful Do's and Don'ts for the Bereaved

Do seek support that caters to the LGBT community as non-LGBT bereavement support groups may not be sensitive to your needs.

Do be supportive of yourself.

Do encourage yourself to express your feelings of sadness.

Do find support wherever you can get it.

Do be kind to yourself and forgiving.

Do recognize that the people around you might have trouble saying "tactful" things.

Do recognize your anger if you feel anger over the loss. It is a normal and natural response.

Do give yourself permission to grieve in your own time, in your own way.

Don't be too harsh on yourself with high expectations of where you "should" be or "might" be emotionally. You are where you are at that point in time, subject to change.

Don't chastise yourself if you cry too much.

Do know it's ok to express your thoughts in writing in this workbook or talk into a tape recorder about your feelings. You don't have to listen back to it, it is designed to just help you vent.

Do know that it is normal to feel all the stages of loss at once and not necessarily in "neat" order.

Do know that you will move around a lot emotionally in your feelings and that your feelings are not "right" and not "wrong", they are just your feelings.

Do know that it is OK to cry, and sometimes feel like screaming.

Don't judge yourself too harshly for any reaction, know that it is subject to change.

Helpful Do's and Don'ts for Friends and Family of the Bereaved

Don't assume that the community resources that are in place for the heterosexual community are in place for the LGBT community regarding loss and grieving.

Do be sensitive to the fact that someone is grieving, hurting and feeling sad, so that recognizing their feelings is a valuable thing to do.

Do be less concerned about the non-traditional relationship and respectful of the fact that the person is hurting and needs to be comforted.

Do be validating of the feelings associated with grief, regardless of the relationship.

Do recognize that no one can totally understand the pain of another, but listening with an attentive ear can be a gift.

Do know that although the general community might not be as supportive as you would hope, the loss is tremendous to the person who is suffering the loss of their loved one.

Don't ask too many questions. Sometimes the best service a friend can provide is to listen and be quiet.

Do know that there may be less "organized" support groups for this grief, but that people need to grieve in their own way and have space and acceptance for their grieving.

Do put aside your own biases and respect the person who is grieving, mourning and needing to express their feelings about their loss.

Do know that even if you as a support person or member of the family have trouble with "accepting" the non-traditional relationship; that the loss is terrible for the person suffering and that they need comfort and a non-judgmental attitude around them.

Don't allow your own feelings of prejudice to interfere with some genuine responses, such as: I know you are hurting and I am sorry for that.

Do ask, is there anything I can do to help to make your grieving easier? Do you need me to listen?

RESOURCES:

The Lesbian, Gay,
Bisexual and Transgender Community Center

Established in 1983, the New York-based Lesbian, Gay, Bisexual & Transgender Community Center has grown to become the largest LGBT multi-service organization on the East Coast and second largest LGBT community center in the world.

Doneley Meris, M.A., C.T. (Masters in Bereavement Counseling; Certified Thanatologist/Death Educator) is their Team Leader for Outreach and Education, Center CARE. Challenges for the LGBT community over grieving and healing are dependent on sensitive and inclusive grief LGBT-focused support groups according to Meris", who also maintains a bereavement psychotherapy practice in New York City where the focus of his work primarily is to meet the challenges of the LGBT bereaved community(ies).

"The LGBT community today continues to face discrimination in more mainstream venues for (bereavement) services," says Meris. "When you add HIV/AIDS into the mix, the sexual orientation and the stigma attached to AIDS become major barriers to the comfort level, trust, and safety of LGBT individuals who attempt to participate in service programs that are not LGBT identified or sensitive. Secondly, there are many institutions that provide grief services that have not had sufficient and realistic trainings working with the LGBT bereavement population.

"There is sensitivity and humaneness specially required of any service practitioner in order to effectively move the healing process for this unique group of individuals. The big elephant of homophobia and heterosexism even in death has to be dealt with to be effective in providing quality grief services."

According to Meris, grief counseling, however, is provided in more and more venues. "Association for Death Education and Counseling (ADEC) has been very actively engaging and encouraging funeral homes, hospital chaplains, hospices, churches, HIV/AIDS service agencies, and other mental health and community-based organizations to incorporate grief services particularly to LGBT individuals in their service provision. Various websites have sprung up that address the unique grief challenges of the LGBT community."

Challenges for the LGBT Community

Challenges for the LGBT community over grieving and healing are dependent on sensitive and inclusive grief LGBT-focused support groups according to Meris. Major cities have been able to address this concern by facilitating support groups but Middle America still needs to incorporate this unique service to the LGBT community which is a major challenge as religion, morality, and politics often get in the way. Other challenges include:

"Grief counseling and support to the LGBT elderly community. Incorporation of grief services into LGBT - queer studies programs. Inclusion of more grief and LGBT presentations in professional organization conferences. Psychoeducational vs. Psychodynamic support group curricula. Funding for LGBT-focused grief supportive services and programs. The government is NOT sensitive to this (triple stigma of LGBT, HIV/AIDS and Death) comes in the way to political advocacy even within the LGBT community political and wellness movement."

Additional information is available from the Lesbian, Gay, Bisexual & Transgender Community Center located at 208 West 13th Street, New York City 1001. They can be contacted at 212-620-7310, or visit their web

site at www.gaycenter.org;
email:gaycenter@gaycenter.org.

National Association of Lesbian, Gay, Bisexual and Transgender Community Centers

The National Association offers links to a variety of LGBT national organizations and resources. There are over 140 community centers throughout the country, with new centers forming every day.

Community centers provide a wide range of programs and services including support groups. Log on to their web site at: www.lgbtcenters.org and going to the directory via an interactive search engine. Or, a hardbound directory is available by: sending $5 and your name and address to NALGBTCC Directory, 12800 Garden Grove Boulevard, Suite F, Garden Grove, CA 92843. Make checks payable to NALGBTCC. For more information on this organization, visit their web site at: www.lgbtcenters.org/directory.asp

Association of Gay and Lesbian Psychiatrists

A community of psychiatrists that educates and advocates on gay, lesbian, bisexual and transgender mental health issues, The National Office of AGLP can provide the names of Psychiatrists (M.D.'s) in your immediate area. These referrals are published in an interactive directory available at:

https://mmm701.vwh1.net/aglpor/cgi-local/referral.cgi.

4514 Chester Avenue
Philadelphia, PA 19143-3707
215-222-2800 (Voice) 215-222-3881 (FAX)
Web site: www.aglp.org

Gay and Lesbian Medical Association

GLMA is a national organization committed to ensuring equality in health care for lesbian, gay, bisexual and transgender (LGBT) individuals and health care professionals. The Gay and Lesbian Medical Association can provide contacts for mental health in your immediate area. These referrals are published in an interactive directory at http://services.glma.org/referrals.

459 Fulton Street, Suite 107
San Francisco, CA 94102
415-255-4547 (Voice) 415-255-4784 (FAX)
E-mail: info@glma.org; Web site: www.glma.org

Gay and Lesbian National Hotline

The Gay and Lesbian National Hotline is dedicated to meeting the needs of the gay, lesbian, bisexual and transgender (GLBT) community. They offer free and confidential peer-counseling, information, and local resources for cities and town throughout the United States. They also maintain the "largest resource database of its kind in the world, with over 18,000 listings." The database contains information on social and support groups as well as gay-friendly religious organizations.

2261 Market Street, PMB # 296

San Francisco, CA 94114

Hotline: 1-888-THE-GLNH (1-888-843-4564)

In New York, call 212-989-0999; San Francisco, call: 415-355-0999

www.glnh.org; E-mail: glnh@glnh.org

Rainbow Resource Directory for Los Angeles County

http://www.resourcedirectory.com/products/directory.php - A comprehensive Resource and Referral Guide to "People Who Can Help" in every community in Los Angeles County, it lists services available in every category. The Rainbow Resource Directory by Glenda Riddick can be obtained by calling, (310) 834-4000, or writing the Resource Directory Group, Inc., 1330 East 223rd Street, Suite 523, Carson, CA 90745.

For information outside California, contact the United Way office in that area or online at http://national.unitedway.org/contact.

Metropolitan Community Churches

The Metropolitan Community Churches is a worldwide fellowship of Christian churches with a special outreach to the world's gay, lesbian, bisexual and transgender communities. There are approximately 200 LGBT-friendly MCC churches in the US and 250 worldwide. A complete list, along with addresses, service times, web sites, phone numbers, clergy info, etc. can be found at www.MCCchurch.org.

8704 Santa Monica Blvd. 2nd Floor
West Hollywood CA 90069- 4548
310- 360- 8640 Fax: 310- 360- 8680
E-mail: info@MCCchurch.org;
Website: www.MCCchurch.org

Shanti

Shanti provides education, practical assistance, and emotional support to people in need and shares its 30 years of experience with organizations nationwide through its training and consultation programs.

Key to the success of Shanti's mission is the *Shanti Model of Peer Support,* which is both a philosophy and a set of techniques that are used throughout their work.

730 Polk Street
San Francisco, CA 94109
(415) 674-4700
http://www.shanti.org

The Gay & Lesbian Center

All lesbian and Gay Seniors (50+) are invited to become a part of the new "Phone Buddy Program". Lesbian and Gay seniors are trained, supervised and available to provide emotional support for grieving the loss of a loved one through friendship over the phone. For more

information contact John Fournier at (323) 860-5830 or online at:
www.la4seniors.com/los_angeles_senior_centers.htm

L.A. Gay and Lesbian Center
The L.A. Gay and Lesbian Center supports the well-being of lesbians and gay men by providing essential human services such as HIV testing, AIDS care, prevention, education, individual, couples and group counseling.

1625 N. Schrader Blvd.
Los Angeles, CA 90028
(323) 993-7400

Aids Project L.A./Mental Health
Aids Project L.A. offers mental health program for clients and their loved ones. Crisis intervention, individual, couple and family counseling, literature, support groups and referrals to treatment.

3550 Wilshire Boulevard, Ste. 300
Los Angeles, CA 90010
(213) 201-1467

8.

Pennies from Heaven

DIVIDENDS HAPPEN IN the most unexpected ways. Normally, we open a bank account and may regularly put small amounts in it. Often, the small child is taught by his mother early about savings ... maybe taken to the bank when she had banking to do. A new name on a new account is exciting ... and so is watching the pennies grow and learning about interest.

Later in life, we may find a penny on the street. It is a small amount, but we may still remember the excitement of watching the account grow. Today, a penny has lost its meaning in gainful spending ... but we may still recall with pleasure the feeling of unanticipated surprise if there is a shiny penny in our path on the street.

There are many "signs" from our loved ones "on the other side" if we're open to them. It may be as simple as a special song on the radio or as complicated as a gift from someone who could never have guessed what the object meant to you in connection to a loved one. A bird that acts "different" than the other birds, a butterfly that hangs around somewhere other than your flowers, a note written before the death that turns up in an unlikely place; sounds, odors, feeling a touch, or something as silly as a turnip coming up in a flower bed. They're all "dividends."

"My skepticism vanished when I spotted and retrieved my first penny," says Steve. "My late wife had been urging me to get into an exercise program, but in my deepest period of depression, exercise was unthinkable. But then, circumstances altered my attitude. Suffering from severe arthritis in both knees caused me to enter a physical rehab program. After getting into the 'swing' of the program my therapist told me to consider swimming as an adjunct to my therapy, so I joined a swim club.

"On my very first lap in the pool I spotted a penny in my lane at the deep end of the pool and felt compelled to dive down and pick it up. It was the first of <u>eleven</u> pennies I collected while swimming or working out in the weight room.

"Many weeks before the episodes at the Club I had found a penny on the floor board of my car on the passenger side, I found one while getting into my car in the garage, one on my townhouse patio and even one on the floor in front of my seat on a flight to Phoenix. After the swimming experience I did indeed become a believer in the 'Pennies from Heaven' phenomenon and that belief was enhanced and validated when I found out that others in my bereavement support group too had their own penny 'finds.'

"After a while the frequency of the 'finds' diminished but then a year and a half into my period of grief I met a wonderful woman in our grief group, a friendship which was to grow into a committed relationship. My new and dear friend and I traveled to Hawaii, stayed at a wonderful Bed & Breakfast, and there while having breakfast on the lanai I spotted a penny on the deck behind a chaise lounge, an area that was cleaned daily. Subsequently I have found pennies in my companion's car and twice at the side of her bed.

"All in all over the last thirty-one months since my beloved wife of fifty-four years died I have found more than twenty-three pennies! I am absolutely convinced that there is much, much more to "Life and Death" than we will ever know."

Or, perhaps, not a penny, but a plum ...
"When Rick and I married," said Gloria, "his daughters gave us a Santa Rosa plum tree, this fruit being Rick's absolute favorite. Rick passed away almost three years ago, in the spring. This tree does, of course, become bare during the winter. Last spring, as the weather began to turn warmer, the tree started to develop new leaves and blooms which would eventually become fruit, but had yet to form. One morning I was in my backyard and happened to glance at this particular tree. Right there, in the middle of blooms that had yet to open, was one, just one fully formed plum hanging from one of the branches. I knew it wasn't left over from last year because the tree had been totally bare all winter. My choice was to believe

that this was a very special plum indeed, one sent as a loving sign from my late husband. I smiled, looked out into the heavens and mouthed a silent thank you to my precious Rick."

Or, a note ...

"There was only one time when I felt my late husband's presence," says Geri. "It was right after he passed away. In fact, I was getting ready for the funeral. And there was one person I knew he was close to, a recovering alcoholic for whom he had been a sponsor. And I knew that this man would want to know my husband had died, but I couldn't find his phone number anywhere. I had my niece over and we both looked and neither of us could find it. The day before the funeral, there it was, taped on the desk right in front of me, in plain sight."

Or, even a first date ...

"I met Gloria as she was saying farewell, having completed a period of time in the grief support group I attended," said Hal. I was tremendously impressed with her farewell comments to the members of her group and ultimately we chatted after the group session. As a professional person, she gave me her business card and at a point further down the road, six months later, I contacted her and asked her out to dinner.

"It's kind of funny how our first 'date' came to pass. I, as so many people, especially the men and some of the women who are grieving, had become a total slob. Not in my personal habits, but as far as keeping a neat and tidy office, I was just slovenly and was extremely neglectful of filing things away. At any rate I had on my desk a huge pile of accumulated documents and papers and bills and so on. I had placed Gloria's business card at the bottom of this pile that kept building month after month.

"One morning I was looking for a particular document and while thumbing through all of the mess on my desk, her business card just flipped out from underneath this eight-inch stack of paperwork and fell on the floor. I picked it up and almost immediately sent her an e-mail saying that I wanted to talk to her (my pretext, because this was a new thing for me, about a business idea that I knew she had some experience in) and that I would like to take her out to dinner. I thought it was very provident that the card had seemed to appear on it's own by flipping onto the floor."

Or, a book ...

"I had been ill for several days with a bad cold. One night I was reading in bed before going to sleep," says Clare. "I became very sleepy, closed the book and set it next to me on the night table. The next morning I reached for the book. It was gone. I looked all around the night table, under the night table, and all around the bedroom. No book. I was baffled."

Clare's housekeeper arrived later that morning and set about cleaning the house, including the bedroom. "A while later," says Clare, "she came to me holding the book I had been searching for. I asked her 'Where did you find it?' She answered that she had found it inside the cover on my late husband's pillow. In order for me to have put that book inside that pillow cover, I would have had to get out of bed, walk over to his side, taken the pillow off the bed and put the book inside the cover." At first, this was disturbing to Clare as she had no idea what to make of it.

"I am now convinced that my late husband came back to give me a sign that he wanted me to know that he was still 'here,' something we had always told each other we would do when one of us passed away. Although I didn't believe in those things before, I am now convinced that that was a sign that he was still taking care of me. Ultimately it did give me comfort because I wasn't feeling well and when that happened I missed my late husband even more than usual. It was his way of sending me comfort."

Or, a comforting smile...

"My wife passed away in the spring of 2002," says Robert, "and this loss has been very difficult for me. However, right after my wife died I had a dream in which she came to me, sat on the bed and just smiled at me. I felt that she was okay, which gave me comfort."

Penny by penny...

"I was with a good friend, leaving her house to go shopping, not long after her husband passed away," says Francine. "As we were walking out of the living room she looked down, saw a penny on the floor and picked it up. She turned to me, smiled, and explained that when you find a penny someone from heaven is sending you their love. She held the penny in her hand and said 'I love you' to her late husband."

"My beloved and I knew that we would soon part due to her terminal disease. We assured each other that who died first would try, if possible, to send pennies to the other," says Clark. "My wife passed away on the first of October and on the first day of each month I always find a bright, shiny, new penny. I find them in the oddest of places. In a pair of shoes that I have not worn in years, on the floor of my car, lying by the front door of my house which no one uses, even tucked into a jacket I haven't worn for years."

True pennies from heaven, all.

9.

A Time for Grief
Religious Rituals of Comfort

GRIEVING IS ABOUT time and a willingness to take responsibility for your own recovery. Every organized religion provides rituals for mourning the loss of loved ones in order to give definition, and hopefully, manageability to our grief. Most embrace a specific timetable for grief, which may or may not mirror your own grief and recovery.

At a time in your life when you are surrounded by uncertainty, patterns that are familiar and structured lend comfort. All religions provide this, whether it is the wake or the shiva. Structure gives us something to do, a routine to follow when one can barely think, and a community to surround us with support and love. In this way, we are not grieving alone.

Regardless of which religion speaks to you emotionally and intellectually, comfort can be found in all. Meet Joette, whose late husband was a Jewish Rabbi. She is a religious woman who has always enjoyed the traditions and celebrations of their faith.

"Although my husband has now been gone for almost three years," says Joette, "some days it seems he was here just yesterday, at other times, I feel I've been alone for so very long." It's even hard to remember, she says, what it was like to live with someone, as she is often lonely and wants to have him there with her. "I have a drawer with some of his clothing and every once in a while I still go to it to embrace his smell.

"I think that a connection to religion gives us something that's bigger than our individual selves, and that's important to me. Am I saying that God has a plan for each of us? I don't know." She wavers in how personally connected she feels to God, but loves Judaism and all the rituals and celebrations that are involved with it. "I like having a connection to my religious life, but the God part, I'm not always so sure of." Her relationship to God is not necessarily the same as her relationship to her religion. "I don't feel that God is directly connected to everything that happens to people."

Since her husband's death, she has given more thought to God and His role in our lives. "It's on my mind more, even though I haven't come up with answers yet. I have more questions but not more answers." She is certain, however, that observing the religious traditions surrounding death, and attending a non-religious bereavement support group have helped heal her grief.

"Am I finished grieving?" she wonders. "I don't need as many tissues to get through the day," is her answer.

Joette lives in California, but because the family has a burial plot in New York, her husband's body was sent there, for a memorial service and burial. "I sat shiva in New York first, but finished the official seven days in California. So I was able to have the comfort of twice-daily prayers with friends and family on both coasts."

She also found that the religious timetables of mourning were beneficial because as each period of time ended, it was as if her religion was encouraging her to go on to the next stage of mourning and healing. "It gave my mourning structure, if you will." As it turned out the mourning period ended just as she was scheduled to return to her work as a teacher, following a school break. "I found that when I was at work I was able to focus completely on my students." And although she doesn't think she did her best job setting up the classroom before the children returned to school, "Once the kids were in the classroom, I was completely focused on them and had no periods of sadness." At the end of the school day, everything changed. "My heart went right back to, 'Oh my gosh, now I'm going to go home and nobody's going to be there.'"

Because of her level of involvement with her Synagogue, and with her many friends there, she has been invited to someone's house for Shabbat dinner, a religious observance, almost every Friday since her husband's passing. She also goes to religious services every Saturday morning and observes Shabbat lunch afterward.

"Did the religious aspects of my life make mourning easier? While it didn't shorten the time it took to work through mourning and healing, I think it did affect my grieving process in a positive way by offering comfort and structure."

The following is a brief overview of various religions and how each structures death and bereavement:

Baha'i

Baha'i dead must be buried within an hour's travel distance from the place of death. Baha'i's do not embalm or cremate their dead. The dead body is washed and wrapped in a shroud. Baha'i's are often buried wearing a Baha'i burial ring. The only ceremonial requirement of a funeral is the recitation of the Prayer for the Dead.

Buddhism

In early times and commonly today, Buddhists cremate the bodies of their dead. The first seven days after death are the most important for final and funereal prayer. Prayers are said weekly, during a 49-day funeral period. These prayers are believed to help the deceased during the post-death transformation and awaken their spirit to the true nature of death. While the primary Japanese Buddhist mourning rituals occur during this period, there are exceptions according to Dennis Klass, professor of religion at Webster University. If there's "something unsettled" about the death—such as an unsolved airline crash or murder, the mourner will say "my 49 days are not over." This sense of non-resolution, Klass says, is echoed by families of murder victims who can't move beyond mourning until legal proceedings are finished.

Catholicism

The Catholic funeral service is called the Mass of the Resurrection. During it, Jesus Christ's life is remembered and related to that of the deceased. Eulogies may be delivered as part of the funeral mass, at a wake, or other non-religious ceremony. There is also a final graveside farewell, and additional traditions depending on the region. The Church encourages Catholics to be buried in Catholic cemeteries. In 1963, the Vatican lifted the ban on cremation for Catholics. However, the remains must be interred, not scattered or kept at home. The community and the church support mourners through the funeral mass and through non-religious services such as wakes.

Eastern Orthodox

The Eastern Orthodox hold a special vigil over the dead called the *parastasis* or *panikhida*, as a time of contemplation on death. The funeral service includes hymns, chants, and Bible readings. Burial is preferred but the Orthodox Church allows cremation if the law of the country requires it. Orthodox Christians pray special prayers for the departed asking God to have mercy on the souls of the dead.

Hinduism

Hindus generally cremate their dead. In preparation, the body is bathed, laid in a coffin, adorned with sandalwood paste and garlands, and wrapped in white cloth. In the cremation ceremony, the body is carried three times counterclockwise around the pyre, and then it is placed upon it. The chief mourner activates the cremation apparatus. The days of mourning are considered a time of ritual impurity. Mourners cover all religious pictures in the house and do not attend festivals, visit swamis or take part in marriage ceremonies. Mourning periods vary in length, though Hindu scriptures caution against excessive mourning.

Islam

The corpse is bathed, wrapped in a plain cloth (called a kafan). The deceased is buried in the ground after the funeral service. Only burial in the ground is allowed according to Shari' ah (Islamic law). Mourners gather and offer prayers for the forgiveness of the deceased. Once the body is buried, Muslim mourners offer one final prayer.

Judaism

The dead are buried as soon as possible. The body is washed to purify it and dressed in a plain linen shroud. The casket, a plain wooden coffin, remains closed after the body is dressed. The body is watched over from time of death till burial, as a sign of respect. The Kaddish, a prayer in honor of the dead, is said. There is an intense seven-day mourning period, called shiva, following the burial.

Mourners traditionally rip their garments as a symbol of grief. Today, people often wear a black ribbon instead of tearing their clothes. Mourners also cover mirrors, sit on low stools, and avoid wearing leather. The full mourning period lasts a year, after which mourners observe the dead's yahrzeit, or yearly anniversary of the death.

Lutheran

There is usually a funeral burial service for the dead. The service takes place in a church, but can also be held in a private home, funeral home or crematory, if desired. A last viewing precedes the funeral service, before which the funeral coffin is closed. Mourners may also be invited to pray at the burial site, and those nearer to the grave may throw handfuls of earth onto the coffin as it descends into the earth.

Mormonism

Funeral services are usually held in an LDS chapel or mortuary. Burial is preferred to cremation because internment in the earth symbolizes the return of dust to dust. The gravesite of the deceased is viewed as a sacred place for the family to visit and tend.

Pagan

Believers in pagan goddess traditions wash the dead body with a mixture consisting of spring water, a few drops of ocean water (or water from another special place), scented oil, and the herb rosemary for purity and protection. While washing, a special blessing is usually said. Then, the body is smudged (or censed) with appropriate incense for the cleansing. Finally, the body is wrapped or dressed in simple cloth or clothing. Pagans hold funerals and memorial services, during which, special prayers are said to help guide the dead to healing in their afterlife journey to rebirth. Rituals include offerings to nature and to ancestors, invoking spirits, and include music, chanting, sharing stories and more.

Presbyterianism

Most funerals take place two to four days after the death. Most services are held in the church sanctuary. Funeral practices vary from person to person. No one form of interment is either encouraged or discouraged, but worshipers are encouraged to provide the "ministry of presence" to those who have experienced a loss. Whether one calls, writes or visits the bereaved, any expression of being present for them is enough.

10.

Organizations and Support Groups

Find bereavement support groups by looking in your local yellow pages, inquiring at your house of worship, internet search engines, hospitals, social service departments, and social service agencies.

The American Academy of Bereavement
http://www.bereavementacademy.org
The American Academy of Bereavement (AAB), a non-profit organization founded in 1993, is a national association devoted to the education, preparation and advancement of bereavement specialists. AAB serves as a stepping stone for professional and personal growth in the field of bereavement. AAB members have the opportunity to establish relationships with colleagues across the country.

AARP

AARP Grief and Loss Programs are available nationally. AARP Grief and Loss Program volunteers provide outreach and emotional support and work closely with community partners to build programs that meet the individual needs of their community. Programs, resources, and services can be adapted to include the loss of a spouse, a parent, sibling or adult child. Many publications and services are available free of charge to the general public. For a more detailed description of each program option contact: AARP Grief and Loss Programs, 601 E Street, NW, Washington, DC 20049. Or, send an email to griefandloss@aarp.org.

AARP Grief Support Line: Toll Free 1-866-797-2277: 9 am - 9 pm ET, Daily

The AARP website, www.aarp.org/griefandloss, offers helpful information on the following:

When the Unexpected Happens
For unexpected and traumatic deaths that can create different obstacles in the grief process.

Where Are You in the Grief Process?
Understanding the process of mourning and the seven steps of grief.

Featured Program: Bereavement Outreach

This Bereavement Outreach Program is a one-to-one peer outreach program in which trained volunteers who have experienced the same type of personal loss help the newly bereaved with both emotional and practical needs.

Final Details
In the first few months, many papers and steps need to be taken. Learn more about these action steps.

Getting Legal Help
When a family member dies, a good lawyer can aid the family in solving many legal questions. Choose one carefully.

Consider A Support Group
Support groups offer us a chance to talk and listen to others, but they may not be right for everyone. Learn if they are right for you.

Men Don't Cry
Many cultures and societies tell us, "Big boys don't cry." That simply isn't—and shouldn't—be true.

Join the Discussion!
Help yourself and others by sharing experiences and reflections on their message boards.

Coping With Your Loss Discussion
One of the most powerful areas of the AARP online community. Share in the challenges of others who are

grieving the loss of a loved one. Post questions, exchange ideas, and gain support.

Coping With the Holidays
Trying to cope with loss and pain can be particularly difficult during the holiday season, but there are ways to express our connection with the loved ones who are no longer here.

Ways to Remember
Discover ways to honor deceased loved ones in ways that are comforting and meaningful.

Customs of Bereavement
Learn about ways other cultures honor their deceased loved ones and express their grief.

AARP PUBLICATIONS:
AARP Grief and Loss Programs Publications:
AARP also provides a variety of information and suggestions in brochure form.

On Being Alone: A Guide for the Newly Widowed — A comprehensive guide for recently widowed men and women, including the experiences of other widows and widowers.

Final Details: A Helpful Guide for Survivors When Death Occurs — Information on making decisions and taking action in the first few months after a death.

Understanding the Grief Process — Basic information about grief and the many ways we grieve the loss of a loved one. Also contains information helpful to family members and friends wanting to be of assistance.

Men and Grief — Special challenges faced by men grieving the loss of a loved one.

Special Issues for Younger Widowed Persons — Offers guidance and support to the younger widow or widower including practical issues and community aftercare resources.

Coping With Celebration Days — Coping strategies for difficult family celebrations after the death of a loved one .

When a Parent Loses a Spouse — Information to adult children whose parent has lost a spouse including ways an adult child can assist their parent, and where to get other help.

ADDITIONAL SUPPORT

ADEC
(Association for Death Education and Counseling)
342 North Main Street
West Hartford, CT 06117-2507
(860) 586-7503 Fax: (860) 586-7550
E-mail: info@adec.org.
Web site: http://www.adec.org

ADEC is one of the oldest interdisciplinary organizations in the field of dying, death and bereavement. The almost 2000 members are made up of a wide array of mental and medical health personnel, educators, clergy, funeral directors, and volunteers. ADEC offers numerous educational opportunities through its annual conference, courses and workshops, its certification program, and via its newsletter, *The Forum*.

Center for Death Education and Bioethics

Dr. Robert A Bendiksen, Director,
Department of Sociology/Archaeology, University of Wisconsin-La Crosse – 435 NH
1725 State St.
La Crosse, WI 54601-3723
(608) 785-6784, FAX (608) 785-8486
E-mail: cdeb@uwlax.edu
Web site:
http://www.uwlax.edu/sociology/cde&b/index.html
The Center for Death Education and Bioethics (CDEB) is a resource center for academic materials concerned with the issues of death, dying and bereavement in contemporary society. Brochures available include "Understanding the Experience of Grief," an explanation of human responses to death.

Grief and Loss Resource Center

Box 1290,
Golden, BC, V0A 1H0
E-Mail: cef@rockies.net

Web site: http://www.rockies.net/~spirit/grief/grief.html
This site is dedicated to grief and bereavement and provides resources for ministers, police, EMS personnel, doctors, nurses, counselors, and other professionals are provided.

Center for Grief Recovery
1263 W. Loyola Ave.
Chicago, IL 60626
773-274-4600
E-mail: information@griefcounselor.org
Web site: http://www.griefcounselor.org/
The Center for Grief Recovery is both a Counseling Center and an idea factory for developing new methods and services. They have sections listing services related to grief and loss at http://www.griefcounselor.org/grief-recovery-spouse-loss.html.

H.O.P.E. UNIT FOUNDATION FOR BEREAVEMENT, LOSS AND TRANSITION

(Hope-Opportunity-Participation-Education)
818-788-HOPE (4673)
Web site: http://www.hopeunit.org
H.O.P.E. offers weekly support groups for widows/widowers for the first two years of mourning, family loss group, and alumni groups for people over two years of mourning. Led by licensed therapists, it the oldest, largest and most professionally run non-profit non-denominational organization and support group in the greater Los Angeles area.

Hospice Foundation of America
800-854-3402 Mon-Fri, 8-6 EST
http://www.hospicefoundation.org/griefAndLoss/
Hospice Foundation of America offers information on the challenges of coping with grief for the bereaved and their support network..

Discussing grief and bereavement during HFA's National Bereavement Teleconference, Cokie Roberts, of ABC News, commented, "Over time, people learn to live with the loss, but it's not something you get over. The grieving process is a series of ups and downs, and often it's more intense in the early years. The thing that we need to remember is that you never have to like a loss. You just have to learn to accept it and deal with it."

This site also explores many of the "Myths" and "Realities" of grief.

The Elizabeth Kubler-Ross Center
South Route 616
Head Waters, VA 24442
(703) 393-3441
http://www.elisabethkublerross.com/pages/AboutGrief.html
Elizabeth Kubler-Ross, M.D. was a psychiatrist and the author of the groundbreaking *On Death and Dying*. She has earned a place as the best-loved and most-respected authority on the subject. "My goal was to break through the layer of professional denial that prohibited patients from airing their inner-most concerns," she wrote.

"Grief is a process of physical, emotional, social and cognitive reactions to loss. The grieving process is hard to work through! One needs to be patient with themselves or others experiencing loss. Although responses to loss are as diverse as the people experiencing it, patterns of stages commonly experienced have emerged. People in grief forget that grief is a process and that through this process, new coping skills are learned."

Eldercare Locator:
A public service of the U.S. Administration on Aging.
The Eldercare Locator connects older Americans and their caregivers with sources of information on senior services. Contact an Eldercare Locator information-specialist by calling 1-800-677-1116

INTERNET BEREAVEMENT SUPPORT

http://www.griefnet.org - offers resources related to death, dying, bereavement, and major emotional and physical losses.

http://www.webhealing.com - includes discussion forums, articles, and other resources about healing from loss.

http://www.beyondindigo.com - a collection of articles, advice, online forums, and support resources dealing with end of life issues, grief, and loss.

http://www.journeyofhearts.org/jofh - stories, poems, quotes, and medical information to help in the transition from loss to healing. Offers emotional support and friendship and provides a safe haven for bereaved persons to share their grief.

http://www.alexandrakennedy.com - offers books and resources for grieving effectively, with emphasis on the loss of a parent. Especially important are her Seven Tasks of Grieving.

http://www.aarp.org/life/griefandloss - offers information and interactive resources for people grieving a death.

http://www.griefcompanion.org - offers writings from classical and contemporary sources for people grieving, a sharing board, and reviews of bereavement resources.

http://www.widowwidowersupport.org - information and support for widows, widowers, and others who are grieving over the death of a loved one. Offers helpful do's and don't for those finding it difficult to know what to say or do for the bereaved. According to this site, widows and widowers experience a greater than average use of alcohol and drugs and widowers over 75 have the highest rate of alcoholism in the country.

http://www.healingthehurt.com - share stories, join in online discussions, post memorials, and photographs for those bereaved by suicide..

http://www.heavensconnection.com - Christian ministry offering commentary on dealing with terminal illness and the loss of a loved one.

http://hcd2.bupa.co.uk/fact sheets/mosby factshee ts/Bereavement.html - explains factors that can make a difficult bereavement more likely, such as: being male; several previous bereavements; a history of mental illness, such as depression, anxiety or previous suicide attempts; a dependent relationship with the person who has died, or a relationship where you had troubled or negative feelings about the deceased; low self-esteem; and, a lack of support from family and friends, death due to AIDS or suicide; the death of a co-habiting partner, same sex partner or partner from an extra-marital relationship, where the relationship may not be legally recognized or accepted by family and friends; a death involving murder, legal proceedings or media coverage; deaths where the bereaved may be responsible; situations where a post mortem or an inquest is required; and, more than one death at once (for example, in an accident)

http://www.griefcircle.org - message board for students of bereavement studies.

http://www.phoenix-method.com - offers advice to handle grief, bereavement, divorce, and loss. The Phoenix Method is a simple, powerful and innovative process to heal grief that combines the cutting edge tools of unconscious psychology with the ancient spiritual wisdom of the east.

Association for Death Education and Counseling
http://www.adec.org
A multi-disciplinary professional organization offering death education, bereavement counseling, and care of the dying.

Share Grief
http://www.sharegrief.com
Online grief counseling.

Acumen Bereavement Counseling
http://www.acumen.org.uk
Compassionate, ethical support by email to people who are grieving and mourning a loss.

RealityWorks - Grief Counseling
http://www.realityworks.net
Offers consultation, training, energywork and creative inspiration with a strengths-based approach through seminars and workshops. Located in Colorado

Grief Care Inc.
http://www.griefcare.info

A California-based nonprofit organization committed to providing compassionate counselling, thorough training, education, and consultation with respect to the bereavement process in loss and life transitions.

Cairns Grief Counseling and Support

http://www.angelfire.com/hi5/memories0/cairns.html
Online counseling with chat and group discussions.

Compassion At Work

http://www.compassionatwork.com/
Provides long-term management training for grief and loss issues at the workplace (downsizings, terminal illness, bereavement and violence) and institutionalizes on-site wellness and compassion.

GotTrouble.com: Grief Counseling

http://gottrouble.com/legal/estate_planning/grief.html
A guide to stages of grief and therapy.

Grief and Loss Counseling Online

http://www.angelfire.com/hi5/memories0/
Offers comfort and support to everyone free of fees and charges. Chats and message boards.

Grief Steps

http://www.griefsteps.com/indexa1.htm – offers support for families in transition with chats, courses, free articles online and books and resources to help you with your grief. Contact: maryann@griefsteps.com or call 262.692.3312.

Sunrise at Midnight
http://www.sunriseatmidnight.com/
Tennessee-based grief recovery specialist provides resources, education, training and certification for adults and children to deal with any loss or change.

Precious Gems Counseling Services
http://preciousgems.org/
A not for profit organization that provides bereavement support within minority communities and links to national organizations and resources.

WholeLife Designs
http://www.wholelifedesigns.com
Provides personal loss counseling services including bereavement, workplace changes and divorce in one-on-one or group and corporate settings.

Finkleman Communications Ltd.
http://members.shaw.ca/finkleman/
Counseling, workshops, seminars, and books related to psychodynamics and coping with personal loss.

Hopeseek
http://www.hopeseek.com

Offers a message board, bereavement services after tragedy, loss and grief counseling, and counseling after loss to suicide.

Gili's Place
http://www.gilisplace.com/
Dr. Henya Kagan (Klein), specialist psychologist in bereavement and loss in Houston, Texas. offers publications, and grief notes.

Southwark Bereavement Care
http://www.southwarkbereavement.org.uk
Offers free bereavement support, advice and information. including a self help guide, e-counseling, and advice for young people.

Designed Thinking
http://www.designedthinking.com/Fear/Abuse/Grief/grief.html
Professional assistance for grief issues. Telephone sessions are available.

Edgebrook
http://www.edgebrook.org
A non profit organization offering residential workshops for persons working through issues of grief and loss as well as survivors of physical, sexual, and emotional abuse.

Cruse Bereavement Care
http://www.cruselochaber.freeuk.com

Help with support, counseling, education, advice and information. Counselors available by phone or e-mail. Located in Scotland.

Beginning Experience
http://www.geocities.com/maximumbob3/index.html
Offers a spiritual weekend designed to help the widowed make a new beginning in life. Grand Rapids, Michigan.

Rainbow Resource Directory for Los Angeles County
http://www.resourcedirectory.com/products/directory.ph
p - A comprehensive Resource and Referral Guide to "People Who Can Help" in every community in Los Angeles County. The Rainbow Resource Directory by Glenda Riddick can be obtained by calling, (310) 834-4000 or writing the Resource Directory Group, Inc., 1330 East 223rd Street, Suite 523, Carson, CA 90745.

For resources outside of California, contact the United Way office in that area or online at http://national.unitedway.org/contact.

World Trade Center's
Disaster Victims Crisis Counseling
http://www.TwoCupsOfJoy.com/worldtradecenter.html
Telephone counseling for loss and grief issues.

The Sanctuary
http://thesanctuaryforgrief.org
Dedicated to providing direct service, education and outreach for children, families, communities and

businesses that have experienced the death of a family member, colleague or friend in Westchester, Long Island and the five boroughs of New York City. Services are non-denominational and confidential.

Four Directions
http://www.healthconsultation.org
Grief and crisis consultation. Online interactive chat forum. No charge for initial consultation.

The Fellow Travelers Bereavement, Grief & Loss Site
http://www.griefcounselling.co.uk/
Professional bereavement counseling online. Free information on different types of grief, links to free services and free voice-interactivity for mutual support.

GENERAL INTERNET RESOURCES

Grief Resources Catalog
http://www.griefresourcescatalog.com/home.html
The Grief Resources Catalog is a resource center dedicated to providing grief support products for those who may be grieving the loss of a loved one and for friends, relatives, and grief professionals who want to help someone who is experiencing grief.
Grief Resources Catalog
5021 Vernon Avenue #209
Edina, MN 55436 USA
(952) 922-3469
E-mail: info@griefresourcescatalog.com

BELIEF NET

www.beliefnet.org

BELIEF NET is a multi-faith e-community designed to help you meet your own religious and spiritual needs -- in an interesting, captivating and engaging way. This site is not affiliated with a particular religion or spiritual movement and is not out to convert you to a particular approach, but rather to help you find your own. Beliefnet, Inc. is a privately held company funded by employees, individual investors and Blue Chip Venture Company.

GriefNet.org

www.GriefNet.org

GriefNet.org is an Internet community of persons dealing with grief, death, and major loss. They have 47 e-mail support groups and two web sites and offer an integrated approach to on-line grief support provides help to people working through loss and grief issues of many kinds.

GriefNet is directed by Cendra (ken'dra) Lynn, Ph.D., a clinical grief psychologist, death educator, and traumatologist who lives in Michigan.

GriefNet, operated as a non-profit corporation under the name Rivendell Resources, offers e-mail support groups, articles, books, audio and video cassettes on grief and bereavement, and links to other internet sites dealing with grief and loss worldwide. Also offers "Memorials" where you can leave a tribute to someone dear to you.

http://www.webhealing.com

Offers a place to understand and honor the many different paths to heal strong emotions. Tom Golden, L.C.S.W. of Washington D.C. is a psychotherapist, author, and speaker on the topic of healing from loss.

The Compassionate Friends

www.compassionatefriends.org

Assist families toward the positive resolution of grief following the death of a child of any age and to provide information to help others be supportive. The Compassionate Friends is a national nonprofit organization with no religious affiliation and there are no membership dues or fees.

11.

Funeral Resources

The Funeral Help Page
Funeral Help Program (FHP)
1236 Ginger Crescent
Virginia Beach, VA 23453 USA
877-427-0220
Email:fhp4@cox.net
Web site: http://www.funeral-help.com
Alzheimer's Research Foundation of Virginia. Offers information on what is, and isn't, required by law in regards to funerals, as well as common sales ploys, misconceptions, and downright scams that have driven funeral costs up at a rate several times normal inflation over the past decade.

Funeral Service Center
Funeral.com, Inc.

4495 Lake Ave S. Suite 200
White Bear Lake MN, 55110
E-mail: info@funeral.com
Web site: http://www.funeral.com/funeral/index.jsp

A resource for information regarding funerals and what to expect. Info on lowering funeral costs through the National Funeral Directors Association.

Federal Trade Commission for the Consumer

Offers FUNERALS: A CONSUMER GUIDE, on the following topics: A Consumer Product; Pre-Need; Planning; Prepaying; What Kind of Funeral Do You Want?; "Traditional," full-service funeral; Direct burial; Direct cremation; Choosing a Funeral Provider; Funeral Costs; Embalming; Caskets; Burial Vaults or Grave Liners; Preservative Processes and Products; Cemetery Sites; Veterans Cemeteries; and, Solving Problems.

You can file a complaint with the FTC by contacting the Consumer Response Center by phone, toll-free, at 1-877-FTC-HELP (382-4357); TDD: 1-866-653-4261; by mail: Consumer Response Center, Federal Trade Commission, 600 Pennsylvania Avenue, NW, Washington, DC 20580; or on the Internet at www.ftc.gov, using the online complaint form. Although the Commission cannot resolve individual problems for consumers, it can act against a company if it sees a pattern of possible law violations.

Most states have a licensing board that regulates the funeral industry. You may contact the board in your state for information or help.

For additional information about making funeral arrangements and the options available contact interested business, professional and consumer groups. Some of the biggest are:

AARP Fulfillment

601 E Street, NW
Washington, DC 20049
1-800-424-3410
Web site: www.aarp.org
AARP is a nonprofit, nonpartisan organization dedicated to helping older Americans achieve lives of independence, dignity and purpose. Its publications, Funeral Goods and Services and Pre-Paying for Your Funeral, are available free by writing to the above address. This and other funeral-related information is posted on the AARP website.

Council of Better Business Bureaus, Inc.

4200 Wilson Blvd., Suite 800
Arlington, VA 22203-1838
Web site: www.bbb.org
Better Business Bureaus are private, nonprofit organizations that promote ethical business standards and voluntary self-regulation of business practices.

Funeral Consumers Alliance

33 Patchen Road
South Burlington, VT 05403
1-800-765-0107

FCA, a nonprofit, educational organization that supports increased funeral consumer protection, is affiliated with the Funeral and Memorial Society of America (FAMSA).

Cremation Association of North America
401 North Michigan Avenue
Chicago, IL 60611
(312) 644-6610
Web site: www.cremationassociation.org
CANA is an association of crematories, cemeteries and funeral homes that offer cremation.

International Cemetery and Funeral Association
1895 Preston White Drive, Suite 220
Reston, VA 20191
800-645-7700
Web site: www.icfa.org
ICFA is a nonprofit association of cemeteries, funeral homes, crematories and monument retailers that offers informal mediation of consumer complaints through its Cemetery Consumer Service Council. Its website provides information and advice under "Consumer Resources."

The ICFA answers questions about funeral and cemetery arrangements, cremation, grief and other issues related to the end of life. A Directory of Providers, and Complaint Resolution Services are available at http://www.icfa.org/consumer.html.

International Order of the Golden Rule
13523 Lakefront Drive

St. Louis, MO 63045

800-637-8030

Web site: www.ogr.org

OGR is an international association of about 1,300 independent funeral homes.

Jewish Funeral Directors of America Seaport Landing

150 Lynnway, Suite 506

Lynn, MA 01902

(781) 477-9300

Web site: www.jfda.org

JFDA is an international association of funeral homes serving the Jewish community.

National Funeral Directors Association

13625 Bishop's Drive

Brookfield, WI 53005

800-228-6332

Web site: www.nfda.org/resources

NFDA is the largest educational and professional association of funeral directors.

National Funeral Directors and Morticians Association

3951 Snapfinger Parkway, Suite 570

Decatur, GA 30035

800-434-0958

Web site: www.nfdma.com

NFDMA is a national association primarily of African-American funeral providers.

National Selected Morticians
5 Revere Drive, Suite 340
Northbrook, IL 60062-8009
800-323-4219
Web site: www.nsm.org
NSM is a national association of funeral firms that have agreed to comply with its Code of Good Funeral Practice. Consumers may request a variety of publications through NSM's affiliate, the Consumer Information Bureau, Inc.

Funeral Service Consumer Assistance Program
PO Box 486
Elm Grove, WI 53122-0486
800-662-7666
FSCAP is a nonprofit consumer service designed to help people understand funeral service and related topics and to help them resolve funeral service concerns. FSCAP service representatives and an intervener assist consumers in identifying needs, addressing complaints and resolving problems. Free brochures on funeral related topics are available.

Funeral Service Educational Foundation
13625 Bishop's Drive
Brookfield, WI 53005
877-402-5900
FSEF is a nonprofit foundation dedicated to advancing professionalism in funeral service and to enhancing public knowledge and understanding through education and research.

Web site:
http://www.ftc.gov/bcp/conline/pubs/services/funeral.htm

National Funeral Directors Association
13625 Bishop's Drive
Brookfield, WI 53005-6607
(800) 228-6332 (262) 789-1880
E-mail: nfda@nfda.org
Web site: www.nfda.org

Offers information on the basic elements of grief plus an explanation of common "Myths and Reality" to enable family, friends, religious leaders and other caregivers to have the correct information about grief, thus enabling them to respond more patiently, compassionately and wisely.

12.

Additional Resources

Social Security Administration

www.socialsecurity.gov

Widows/widowers can report the death to a service representative by calling this toll-free number, 1-800-772-1213, between the hours of 7 a.m. and 7 p.m. on business days. Have your Social Security number handy. If you're deaf or hard of hearing, call our toll-free TTY number, 1-800-325-0778, between 7 a.m. and 7 p.m. on business days. If you're getting disability or retirement benefits on your spouse's record when he or she dies, they will change your payments to survivors' benefits. If you're getting benefits on your own record, you may apply for survivors' benefits. This web site offers comprehensive information regarding social security benefits, including the "lump-sum death benefit."

NEWSLETTERS

Bereavement Magazine, a magazine of hope and healing. 8133 Telegraph Drive, Colorado Springs, CO 80920, (719) 282-1948, FAX (719) 282-1850. Andrea Gambil, editor.

Caring Concepts, a coffee break newsletter for caring persons. Centering Corp., 1531 N. Saddle Creek Rd., Omaha, NE 68104-5064, (402) 553-1200.

Grief Steps Newsletter, published weekly is offered free of charge. Sign up by e-mail: ChampLtd-34932@autocontactor.com or visit www.griefsteps.com.

CARING FOR GRIEVING CHILDREN

While the majority of widows/widowers and grieving partners commonly no longer have young children at home, for some this is not the case, such as widows and widowers of military personnel. In grieving our late spouses and partners, if there are young children suffering the loss of a parent, helping these children to heal is a necessary step. To this end, we present the:

MISS Foundation
P.O. Box 5333
Peoria, Arizona 85385
E-mail: information@misschildren.org
Web site: www.misschildren.org

You can help your children who are grieving with these tips from the MISS Foundation:

1. Children need comfort and frequent reassurance that they're safe, loved, and taken care of.

2. Be honest, simple, and direct when talking to them about death.

3. Encourage them to express their feelings through talking, drawing, and playing.

4. Try to maintain a normal routine.

5. Find local children's support groups to help.

6. Avoid telling them that God took their loved one. Avoid associating death with sleep or something 'lost.' Remember children are very literal.

7. Allow them to participate in rituals such as funerals, memorial services, and candle lightings. Children should be offered the opportunity to say goodbye to their loved ones.

8. Encourage questions. Do not discourage them from talking about their pain.

9. Be patient and very gentle with them. Try not to yell at, hit, or isolate them.

MISS also offers this advice:

Common ways in which children may respond to a death include: sadness; denial, shock, and confusion; anger, irritability, and 'bad' behavior; inability to sleep; nightmares or fear of sleep; loss of appetite; fear of being alone; somatic/physical complaints such as stomach aches and headaches; inability to concentrate or focus; guilt over failure to prevent the loss; depression or a loss of interest in daily activities; regressive behavior—acting much younger or reverting to earlier behaviors; withdrawal from friends; sharp drop in school performance; talking frequently and asking repeated questions about the death, or making repeated statements of wanting to join the deceased; and profound emotional reactions."

How to help a grieving child?

Children are physical in their grief process. Interact with them when playing and support their special 'language' of grief expression. Art and writing are particularly helpful.

Young children are concrete thinkers. Avoid expressing such as passed on, at rest, or we lost when talking about the person who died. Be direct and honest. Offer only what they can absorb and keep it simple.

Children can be fearful about death and feel insecurity about their future. Give them a chance to discuss those fears and validate their feelings. Offer the support of another adult they trust as children hesitate talking to their parents about their true grief feelings.

Be patient with the child. Children are not able to express overwhelming sadness into words, so try to interpret perceived behavior problems as manifestations of grief. Be more flexible in punishment and it is suggested that positive reinforcement be employed rather than harsh discipline. Yelling, hitting, or isolating a grieving child can exacerbate the symptoms and creates a vicious cycle for the family.

Keep routines as much as possible. Try not to make any major decisions for 18 months. Children need to be assured that they have security, stability, and love.

Adults can provide a good grief "model" for the grieving child. Share an 'open emotion' policy and allow yourself, and your child, to cry when needed. Your openness will validate their feelings.

Children are intermittent grievers. Just because they don't cry everyday doesn't mean they aren't hurting. Some children cry for one minute and jump right back into normal play.

Expect their grief to revisit during their childhood and through adolescence. Triggers awaken old grief. Make yourself available.

Shower them with affection and attention. If you are feeling too overwhelmed with your own grief, call a friend, a support group, your church, or someone else who can help!

II.

The Healing Power of Thought
Workbook

Introduction
Why do we need a workbook?

PUTTING YOUR THOUGHTS on paper gives you a private place to express your feelings, a place to grieve, and to heal, whether you write poetry, memories, stories, or whether you write letters to your deceased spouse, or simply keep a journal or use this workbook. The writing doesn't have to be perfect and it never needs to be shared. It helps because it gives you a place to store your grief outside of yourself so that painful feelings can be expressed and eventually released.

Writing your thoughts down also provides you with a record as you mourn your late spouse so that you can look back over your journey and take comfort in your progress. As time passes, it is hard to remember how we felt immediately following the death of a spouse, just as it's impossible to re-create in our minds the actual feeling of physical pain. But looking back at what we wrote months before allows us to see our growth in a positive and reassuring way.

Use this workbook to expand your understanding of your own feelings. Our feelings, if misunderstood or unexpressed, stay bottled up inside ourselves without ever becoming clear. At a time when thoughts and feelings are muddy, putting thoughts down on paper provide a clearer path to understanding. Also, recording frequently helps alleviate some stress and anxiety.

Writing is a way of talking to ourselves and magnifying our own thinking. It's a way of making conscious choices about being more positive in our thoughts, of moving away from depressed feelings and into the sunlight of other directions we can take. During the earliest time sequences of grief, when concentration is most difficult, this workbook provides only simple prompts to help you explore your thoughts.. As healing progresses, the prompts become more complex and in-depth, as your ability to explore and respond grows. Some questions and prompts may repeat in various chapters to encourage you to revisit aspects of your mourning in a positive way.

During the process of grieving, others often grow weary of our sadness and tears. They want you to stop grieving, to "get over it" and get on with life. They no longer want to listen to you talk about your loss and pain. But it's just not that easy. Grieving is an individual journey and has no "correct" time schedule. Some days you will feel better than you do on other days. Along with writing your thoughts down, consider joining a bereavement support group, which is often helpful because you are with others who truly understand what you are going through. Together you learn to be patient with the grief process, the sadness and the tears.

As in the time sequences in this book, you may find yourself going through each of the emotional stages in the order we have listed, of shock, denial, anger, depression, and finally, integration, adjustment and transition, stages based loosely on the "stages of grief" first acknowledged by Dr. Elizabeth Kubler-Ross for those "living while dying." Or, you may find yourself jumping all over the place in a forward-and-backward movement. That's okay.

You may seem to skip one stage completely, only to encounter it long after you have thought yourself emotionally healed. How so? Maybe you didn't allow yourself to recognize, for instance, anger directed inward, or directed outward toward your late spouse or even the world-at-large. Those feelings had to wait until you were feeling stronger and in control of your life once again.

You may even go through some of these steps more than once and experience even deeper feelings each successive time. Or, in the course of any one day, you may find yourself in touch with all of these stages. What a day! Mourning is not an exact process; it is loose and fluid and does not fit into a cookie-cutter mold. We encourage you to use this workbook as your mourning and healing dictates by reading the chapter that explores what you are feeling *right now*. When people say that grievers are all in the same boat, it is really that people are in the same water, in different boats, with odd oars.

1.

Time Sequence One
Months One through Four
Shock

THE EARLIEST FEELINGS of mourning include the initial shock (this can't be happening), denial of the reality, feeling overwhelmed and numb. It is not uncommon to feel some loss of self-esteem and to be extremely vulnerable. Symptoms usually include a variety of internal complaints, a great deal of crying, insomnia, waking from sleep or not being able to fall asleep, feeling anxious, loss of appetite, possible sweaty hands and heart palpitations.

You may also experience irritability, lack of patience, forgetfulness, distractibility and loss of concentration. Feelings of sadness and loneliness accompany feeling bewildered.

Shock is your alarm response to a sudden, violent or upsetting disturbance. Whether the loss is sudden or expected, the element of shock is still present. It is an alarm state that protects you from the flood of emotions with which you may be unable to cope. Whether experienced as anxiety, insomnia and/or numbness, it actually helps you to get through this initial time period.

1. What does the emotional pain I wake to each morning feel like?

_____

_____

_____

_____

_____

_____

_____

_____

_____

_____

_____

_____

What do I do to cope with this pain?

_____

_____

_____

_____

_____

_____

_____

_____

_____

_____

_____

_____

2. I am crying a lot because I frequently feel overwhelmed. In order to be less scared, I do the following things:

_____

_____

_____

_____

_____

_____

_____

_____

_____

_____

_____

_____

_____

_____

_____

_____

_____

_____

_____

_____

_____

_____

_____

_____

_____

_____

_____

3. I haven't been able to cry and I would like to, because I imagine I would feel better. I sometimes feel the sensation of tightness in my chestt. When I can't cry and feel tied up in knots, it feels like this:

_____
_____
_____
_____
_____
_____
_____
_____
_____
_____
_____
_____
_____
_____
_____
_____
_____
_____
_____
_____
_____
_____
_____
_____
_____
_____

4. I am afraid to leave my house; I used to be very active, why am I feeling safe only in the confines of my home?

_____

_____

_____

_____

_____

_____

_____

_____

_____

_____

_____

_____

_____

_____

_____

_____

_____

_____

_____

_____

_____

_____

_____

_____

_____

5. *I seem to be running all the time. What am I running from? I am filling every waking moment with frantic activity. What am I trying to avoid?*

_____

_____

_____

_____

_____

_____

_____

_____

_____

_____

If I wasn't running, what would I be doing and how might I feel?

_____

_____

_____

_____

_____

_____

_____

_____

_____

_____

6. I am having a lot of trouble completing even simple tasks. I get distracted. When I start to accomplish something, this is what happens to me:

_____

_____

_____

_____

_____

_____

_____

_____

_____

_____

_____

_____

_____

_____

_____

_____

_____

_____

_____

_____

_____

_____

_____

7. I have trouble getting out of bed. I feel bad and want to stay under the covers and not face the day. Three things I will do for myself to help me "jump-start" my day. Example: exercise or call a friend.

1._____

_____

_____

_____

_____

_____

_____

_____

2._____

_____

_____

_____

_____

_____

_____

3._____

_____

_____

_____

_____

_____

8. *I have a lot of trouble having control over my emotions. I may break down in unexpected places and embarrass myself. Why am I so afraid to cry in public or when I'm with a friend. What do I think would happen if I did?*

_____

_____

_____

_____

_____

_____

_____

_____

_____

_____

_____

_____

_____

_____

_____

_____

_____

_____

_____

_____

_____

_____

9. *Sometimes I don't have an appetite. Other times, I want to eat everything in sight. When I overeat I feel:*

_____

_____

_____

_____

_____

_____

_____

_____

_____

_____

_____

_____

When I can't eat I feel:

_____

_____

_____

_____

_____

_____

_____

_____

_____

_____

10. Often, I am very forgetful. I lose things, or misplace them. When those things happen. I get scared. I am scared about:

_____

_____

_____

_____

_____

_____

_____

_____

_____

_____

_____

_____

_____

_____

_____

_____

_____

_____

_____

_____

_____

_____

_____

_____

11. I feel numb a lot or on "automatic pilot." When I feel numb it feels like:

_____
_____
_____
_____
_____
_____
_____
_____
_____
_____
_____
_____
_____
_____
_____
_____
_____
_____
_____
_____
_____
_____
_____
_____
_____

12. I get scared when I think about what I am going to do with the rest of my life. I know its not wise to go too far ahead. When I get scared, three constructive things I can do for myself are:

1._____

_____

_____

_____

_____

_____

_____

2._____

_____

_____

_____

_____

_____

_____

3._____

_____

_____

_____

_____

_____

_____

_____

13. When I get sick, I get scared about how I will take care of myself. Sometimes, I tell myself scary stories. If I were to tell myself good, safe stories, what would they sound like?

_____

_____

_____

_____

_____

_____

_____

_____

_____

_____

_____

_____

_____

_____

_____

_____

_____

_____

_____

_____

_____

_____

_____

_____

_____

14. I seem to have a lot of fears right now. Here are three ways in which I can calm myself down:

1._____

_____

_____

_____

_____

_____

_____

_____

2._____

_____

_____

_____

_____

_____

_____

3._____

_____

_____

_____

_____

_____

_____

_____

_____

_____

15. I'm not used to traveling alone and taking care of myself. Three ways in which I took care of myself before are:

1._____

2._____

3._____

*16. How do I feel about taking off my wedding ring?
What does it mean to me to take it off?*

_____

_____

_____

_____

_____

_____

_____

_____

_____

_____

_____

_____

_____

_____

_____

_____

_____

_____

_____

_____

_____

_____

_____

_____

17. Some of my family members or friends are urging me to clean out the closets. I'm not ready yet. This is how I feel about it now:

_____

_____

_____

_____

_____

_____

_____

_____

_____

_____

_____

_____

_____

_____

_____

_____

_____

_____

_____

_____

_____

_____

_____

_____

_____

_____

18. I seem to be running all the time. This is how I feel when I am running:

_____

_____

_____

_____

_____

_____

_____

_____

_____

_____

_____

_____

_____

_____

_____

_____

_____

_____

_____

_____

_____

_____

_____

19. I used to be very active. This is how I feel when I am not running:

_____

_____

_____

_____

_____

_____

_____

_____

_____

_____

_____

_____

_____

_____

_____

_____

_____

_____

_____

_____

_____

_____

_____

_____

_____

20. Sometimes I cry at unexpected times, in front of my young grandchildren or grown children. If I could give it words, this is what I would like to say to them:

_____

_____

_____

_____

_____

_____

_____

_____

_____

_____

_____

_____

_____

_____

_____

_____

_____

_____

_____

_____

_____

_____

_____

_____

_____

_____

_____

21. I often feel dependent on others when I am used to feeling independent. If I could give words to it, it would sound like this:

_____

_____

_____

_____

_____

_____

_____

_____

_____

_____

_____

_____

_____

_____

_____

_____

_____

_____

_____

_____

_____

_____

_____

_____

_____

_____

23. I want to feel capable again and don't know how. At other times in my life, I felt capable when:

1._____

_____

_____

_____

_____

_____

_____

_____

2._____

_____

_____

_____

_____

_____

_____

_____

3._____

_____

_____

_____

_____

_____

_____

_____

23. I am anticipating a lot of anxiety when I have to face the first birthday, anniversary or holiday after losing my spouse; three constructive things I will do for myself are:

1._____

_____

_____

_____

_____

_____

_____

2._____

_____

_____

_____

_____

_____

3._____

_____

_____

_____

_____

_____

_____

_____

24. I recognize that not being alone on these days would be good for me. I will have the following plans:

_____

_____

_____

_____

_____

_____

_____

_____

_____

_____

_____

_____

_____

_____

_____

_____

_____

_____

_____

_____

_____

_____

_____

25. Three ways in which I will take care of myself are:

1._____
_____
_____
_____
_____
_____
_____

2._____
_____
_____
_____
_____
_____
_____

3._____
_____
_____
_____
_____
_____
_____
_____

26. Sometimes I feel guilty about being happy again or laughing or smiling. I feel disloyal to my deceased spouse. It is OK for me to smile again and enjoy life. I will make three positive affirmations about myself and they are:

1._____

_____

_____

_____

_____

_____

_____

2._____

_____

_____

_____

_____

_____

_____

3._____

_____

_____

_____

_____

_____

_____

_____

2.

Time Sequence Two
Months Five through Eight
Denial

IN THIS SECOND time sequence of five to eight months, there is often a struggle between holding on and letting go that will create a tension of its own. Ambivalence may show up in a lot of areas; the drive to heal and move on and the need to hold on and stay put. Being accepting of being tugged in two directions, and that these feeling are normal, is helpful. Giving yourself permission to be confused, conflicted and ill at ease is helpful in the continuous process of recognizing feelings and coming to grips with them.

A mind/body approach is useful to manage anxiety. Staying present in the moment, noticing where in your body tension resides, and diminishing it with imagery helps. If there is a "knot" in your shoulder, use your mind to relax it. If there is a boulder on your back, make it smaller. If you are feeling like a hard black rock, make it softer in your mind or change the color. Use the visual part of your mind that is good with creating pictures to help you reduce body tension.

It is important to strive for positive responses in your answers and utilize "reframing," i.e., when something is experienced in a negative way, try to turn it around, to look at "what would help you live with it better," or in an easier way. Reframing means changing the meaning of the behavior, so that you feel differently about it as you work towards introspection and growth and ultimately, healing.

1. How do I honor myself at a time that I feel vulnerable? These are some of the good things that I have going on in my life right now:

_____

_____

_____

_____

_____

_____

_____

_____

_____

_____

_____

_____

_____

_____

_____

_____

_____

_____

_____

_____

_____

_____

_____

_____

_____

2. When I feel overwhelmed, there are some concrete things I can do for myself. I can meditate, listen to relaxation tapes, slow down, go to yoga, exercise, take a walk, run a hot bath, cut roses from my garden or call a friend. These are the things I am choosing to do and why:

_____

_____

_____

_____

_____

_____

_____

_____

_____

_____

_____

_____

_____

_____

_____

_____

_____

_____

_____

_____

_____

_____

_____

_____

3. How can I begin to have a life again? There are three concrete things that I will do in order to put one foot in front of the other and begin:

1._____
_____
_____
_____
_____
_____
_____
_____

2._____
_____
_____
_____
_____
_____
_____

3._____
_____
_____
_____
_____
_____
_____
_____

4. What will my life look like? I might not know but I understand its not good to try to look too far in the future. I will take one day at a time and each day I will have a good attitude. I will help myself in the following ways:

1._____

_____

_____

_____

_____

_____

_____

2._____

_____

_____

_____

_____

_____

_____

3._____

_____

_____

_____

_____

_____

_____

_____

5. There are some days I want to do nothing, on those days I will make an extra effort to get out of bed. I will commit to doing the following three constructive things that day:

1._____

_____

_____

_____

_____

_____

_____

_____

2._____

_____

_____

_____

_____

_____

3._____

_____

_____

_____

_____

_____

_____

6. I have trouble thinking about the future. Knowing that it is best to stay in the "now," I can best do that by breathing, recognizing my negative thoughts but not engaging them, and focusing on what is positive in my life. I will work with myself in the following ways:

_____

_____

_____

_____

_____

_____

_____

_____

_____

_____

_____

_____

_____

_____

_____

_____

_____

_____

_____

_____

_____

_____

_____

7. *My future was going to be with him/her. I have to develop a life for myself when I am still learning what my "self" is. There are three positive things that I know about myself:*

1._____

_____

_____

_____

_____

_____

_____

2._____

_____

_____

_____

_____

_____

3._____

_____

_____

_____

_____

_____

_____

_____

_____

8. Sometimes I think about what I should have done or might have done or could have done at the end of his/her life. I want to get beyond that point. I want to forgive myself for being a less-than-perfect person. Three things I will work on to accomplish that are:

1._____

_____

_____

_____

_____

_____

_____

2._____

_____

_____

_____

_____

_____

_____

3._____

_____

_____

_____

_____

_____

_____

_____

9. I know it is important to stay in the "now."
Frequently I have trouble doing that. If I go to the past, I
am anxious. When I think about the future I am anxious.
How do I stay in the "Now"? By being present with
yourself and being conscious of quiet breathing,
breathing more deeply, gently in and out is a simple way
to begin. The mind will have a lot of thoughts, when
they occur, allow the thought to pass without
attachment, and stay in the moment. *Three times a day I*
will practice staying "present in the moment." I will
note my progress and write down three occasions when
I was able to do this.

1._____

_____

_____

_____

_____

_____

_____

2._____

_____

_____

_____

_____

_____

3._____

_____

_____

_____

_____

10. Sometimes I feel "out of control." I feel upset, that nothing is turning out right. When I have these thoughts, I notice that they can escalate. Three things I will do to slow down these feelings are:

1._____

_____

_____

_____

_____

_____

_____

_____

2._____

_____

_____

_____

_____

_____

_____

3._____

_____

_____

_____

_____

_____

_____

_____

_____

11. I will pay attention to what triggers me and how I might contribute to my own stress. I will reduce my stress in the following ways:

1._____

_____

_____

_____

_____

_____

_____

2._____

_____

_____

_____

_____

_____

_____

_____

3._____

_____

_____

_____

_____

_____

_____

_____

12. I find that my anxiety level is increasing. I want to learn how to work with that. I will become more aware of what causes me anxiety, I will breathe through it, and I will imagine a lighter heart, a chest that is less tense. I will work with my body to calm down. I might imagine the beach or the mountains or any place that gives me pleasure. I am committed to reducing my anxiety. I will do that in the following ways:

_____

_____

_____

_____

_____

_____

_____

_____

_____

_____

_____

_____

_____

_____

_____

_____

_____

_____

_____

_____

_____

_____

*13. My belief system will allow me to lower my anxiety. I will work with a mind and body approach by doing the following:*_____

_____

_____

_____

_____

_____

_____

_____

_____

_____

_____

_____

_____

_____

_____

_____

_____

_____

_____

_____

_____

_____

_____

14. I am not ready for dating. How do people move to be ready to socialize? I am scared, I'm fearful of taking risks. I will allow myself to go slowly and to take one baby step at a time. Often the anticipation is worse than the event. I will talk to myself, I will encourage myself, I will acknowledge that "I am scared" and still know that it is alright for me to go slowly and respect and recognize my feelings. I will encourage myself in the following ways:

_____

_____

_____

_____

_____

_____

_____

_____

_____

_____

_____

_____

_____

_____

_____

_____

_____

_____

_____

_____

_____

15. In some ways I feel worse than at the beginning. I feel worse in the following ways:

_____

_____

_____

_____

_____

_____

_____

_____

_____

_____

_____

_____

_____

_____

_____

_____

_____

_____

_____

_____

_____

_____

_____

_____

_____

16. If I were to allow myself to feel OK, this is what would come up for me, I would imagine:

_____

_____

_____

_____

_____

_____

_____

_____

_____

_____

_____

_____

_____

_____

_____

_____

_____

_____

_____

_____

_____

_____

_____

_____

_____

_____

_____

_____

_____

_____

_____

17. When I think about my future, I feel very uncertain. Three constructive ways that I will think about my future are:

1._____

_____

_____

_____

_____

_____

_____

2._____

_____

_____

_____

_____

_____

_____

3._____

_____

_____

_____

_____

_____

_____

_____

18. I will create "intentions" by developing a list of things I intend to do or become or work towards. I will be very specific:

_____

_____

_____

_____

_____

_____

_____

_____

_____

_____

_____

_____

_____

_____

_____

_____

_____

_____

_____

_____

_____

_____

_____

_____

_____

_____

19. If I think about dating, I feel disloyal to my deceased spouse. He or she would say this to me:

_____

_____

_____

_____

_____

_____

_____

_____

_____

_____

_____

_____

_____

_____

_____

_____

_____

_____

_____

_____

_____

_____

_____

_____

_____

_____

_____

_____

_____

20. Some guidelines I could give myself when I think I might be ready to date. These are the ways that I would encourage myself:

_____

_____

_____

_____

_____

_____

_____

_____

_____

_____

_____

_____

_____

_____

_____

_____

_____

_____

_____

_____

_____

_____

_____

_____

_____

_____

21. My fears about entering the dating world are:

_____

_____

_____

_____

_____

_____

_____

_____

_____

_____

_____

_____

_____

_____

_____

_____

_____

_____

_____

_____

_____

_____

_____

_____

22. I fear that I will spend the rest of my life lonely. Three constructive things I will do for myself are:

1._____

_____

_____

_____

_____

_____

_____

_____

2._____

_____

_____

_____

_____

_____

_____

_____

3._____

_____

_____

_____

_____

_____

_____

_____

_____

23. When my married friends invite me out and I feel like a "5ᵗʰ wheel;" three constructive things I can do for myself are:

1._____

_____

_____

_____

_____

_____

_____

2._____

_____

_____

_____

_____

_____

_____

3._____

_____

_____

_____

_____

_____

_____

_____

24. Three constructive ways in which I can reconstruct and have a better social life are:

1._____

_____

_____

_____

_____

_____

_____

2._____

_____

_____

_____

_____

_____

_____

3._____

_____

_____

_____

_____

_____

_____

25. Sometimes I am afraid that I will forget the joys, hopes, memories ... smiles ... how can I remember the happiness with less pain? What can I do for myself so that I can enjoy the good memories I have without experiencing the extreme sadness?

_____

_____

_____

_____

_____

_____

_____

_____

_____

_____

_____

_____

_____

_____

_____

_____

_____

_____

_____

_____

_____

_____

_____

26. My husband and I did not have a "perfect" relationship and we argued a lot. I have trouble mourning the loss; I am still grieving. Three ways in which I can forgive and help myself are:

1._____

_____

_____

_____

_____

_____

_____

2._____

_____

_____

_____

_____

_____

_____

3._____

_____

_____

_____

_____

_____

_____

_____

27. Some things I would like to tell him are:

_____

_____

_____

_____

_____

_____

_____

_____

_____

_____

_____

_____

_____

_____

_____

_____

_____

_____

_____

_____

_____

_____

_____

_____

_____

28. These are the things I imagine he would say back to me:

_____

_____

_____

_____

_____

_____

_____

_____

_____

_____

_____

_____

_____

_____

_____

_____

_____

_____

_____

_____

_____

_____

_____

_____

_____

29. I very much want to heal. It is important to encourage positive responses in your answers and utilize "reframing". When something was experienced in a negative way, you might want to turn it around and look at "what would help you live with it better" or in an easier way. Reframing means changing the meaning of the behavior, so that you feel differently about it. We are working towards introspection and growth and ultimately, healing. *Three ways that I would encourage myself to heal are:*

1._____
_____
_____
_____
_____
_____
_____

2._____
_____
_____
_____
_____
_____
_____
_____

3._____
_____
_____
_____
_____
_____

3.

Time Sequence Three
Months Nine through Twelve
Anger

Sometimes I don't know what to do with myself. I am angry with the injustice at the death of my spouse. I am angry at the world. "It's not fair." I want to kick and scream like a child. Where did my life go? Why did you leave? (I know I am unreasonable). Why now, as I am getting older, am I left alone? What do I do about this anger? I know I want instant answers when that is not possible. I yearn for calm and serenity when inside I am bottled up with rage and insecurity.

WHEN DENIAL CAN no longer be maintained, feelings of anger, rage, envy and resentment may show up. This anger may be directed outward or inward. Anger toward yourself may look like self-blame, (i.e., "I should have done more … If only I had …") resulting in feelings of guilt, shame, helplessness and fear. When directed outward, there is a danger of becoming caught up in bitterness, resentment and alienation. Instead of feeling sorrow and emotional pain, you may lash out at any convenient scapegoat (i.e., the doctors, god, an inept salesperson, your children, etc.).

It is important to work through your feelings of anger and fear, as well as feelings of guilt and envy.

Few survivors escape without some feeling of guilt. You might feel guilty because you did not make sure your spouse took care of his or her health or got to the doctor sooner. Or you encouraged him or her to attend to a doctor appointment, and they did not. Or, you gave permission for surgery and your spouse didn't recover or you arranged for your spouse to be taken off life support systems. A long illness may have led to a feeling of resentment and consequently guilt over the resentment. A sudden or accidental death may give rise to the torture of all kinds of "if only's."

Anger basically has two directions—outward or inward. Turned outward in healthy grief, it is universally and inevitably directed against the lost partner, even when that person is lost through death. Anger toward your late spouse stems from various sources: previous anger present in the relationship and hostility at that person for dying and leaving you potentially helpless and abandoned.

When anger is expressed outwardly, you commonly project it on other people - anyone who is not suffering in the same way you are. Anger can also be directed toward people who attempt to be comforting because to accept such comfort would be a reminder of the loss and trigger more pain. There are also some people who handle uncomfortable feelings by denying them and lashing out at any convenient scapegoat. Because these feelings are part of grief, you might find yourself "snapping" at others instead of feeling sorrow or pain.

The danger to projecting anger onto others is that you may become caught up in bitterness, resentment, and alienation. After admitting your anger to yourself, write about it. It also helps talk to someone you trust. This may be frightening, but anger accumulates and will erupt eventually, maybe frightening or hurting another person. A good friend may be a good listener or a professional therapist may help you work through your feelings of anger or fear.

Anger expressed inwardly can become depression, for example, anger at yourself for not doing enough or responding fast enough.

When anger builds up to the point of explosion, there are techniques for letting off steam without hurting yourself or others. Pent up emotions are stored in the body and can be released through physical activity: screaming or beating on a pillow, tearing up a telephone book or even throwing stones in the ocean can be helpful. So too are taking long walks, working out in a gym, or swimming. Less physical outlets might include talking into a tape recorder, writing in a personal journal or workbook or drawing pictures that express your feelings. These activities often provide temporary relief by releasing pent up feelings.

Another common, yet difficult to face emotion is envy of a world that seems full of couples, people that can plan trips, buy season tickets for the theatre, go out to dinner, etc., knowing they will always have their spouse to accompany them. It may manifest as anger or suddenly hit like a ton of bricks long past the anger and immediate mourning stage, when you are picking up the pieces of your life and moving ahead. Before the death, you thought that you knew what the rest of your life would look like and that has now forever changed.

Take it one day at a time. Life will be here tomorrow. Use a lot of "self-talk" and safe-guards; learn how to take care of yourself.

1. When I am angry, I know it is OK to express my feelings. I will write them down and later see if they make sense. I am angry about:

_____

_____

_____

_____

_____

_____

_____

_____

_____

_____

_____

_____

_____

_____

_____

_____

_____

_____

_____

_____

_____

_____

_____

_____

_____

2. I am feeling alone and anxious about:

_____

_____

_____

_____

_____

_____

_____

_____

_____

_____

_____

_____

_____

_____

_____

_____

_____

_____

_____

_____

_____

_____

_____

_____

_____

_____

_____

_____

_____

3. *I am feeling more depressed now than I did when my spouse first died. I know this happens a lot, because at first I was so overwhelmed with things to take care of and now, I have time to think. When I think, I get anxious.* Breathe. Meditate. Listen to relaxation tapes. How does doing these things make you feel?

_____

_____

_____

_____

_____

_____

_____

_____

_____

_____

_____

_____

_____

_____

_____

_____

_____

_____

_____

_____

_____

_____

_____

4. As I worry about how my life will be, I will strive to live in this moment of time. Five things I can do for myself to live in this moment of time are:

1._____
_____
_____
_____
_____

2._____
_____
_____
_____
_____

3._____
_____
_____
_____
_____

4._____
_____
_____
_____
_____

5._____
_____
_____
_____
_____
_____

5. I will recover slowly. I will recover if I take one day at a time. I will make the most of each day. When I get overwhelmed, I will remember to BREATHE. I will give myself permission to feel what I feel. If I feel terror, anxiety, worry, doubt or guilt, I will give myself permission to feel it and let it go. I will actively "allow" and "release" these feelings and be less judgmental of myself. I will begin this journey by being mindful of:

_____

_____

_____

_____

_____

_____

_____

_____

_____

_____

_____

_____

_____

_____

_____

_____

_____

_____

_____

_____

6. I don't like feeling like a third wheel when I join couples that we had previously socialized with, yet I get many invitations. Making a decision about socializing with your friends often depends on the mood you are in, and the loneliness factor. *How do I know when I should not accept and when I should? What guidelines will I use?:*

_____

_____

_____

_____

_____

_____

_____

_____

_____

When I get very lonely I take care of myself by:

_____

_____

_____

_____

_____

_____

_____

_____

_____

7. I get torn between wanting to date and staying at home. How will I know when I am ready? I know I want to date/socialize because I have the following feelings:

_____

_____

_____

_____

_____

_____

_____

_____

_____

I get scared of:

_____

_____

_____

_____

_____

_____

_____

_____

When I have confidence, I am in touch with certain qualities within myself; They are:

_____

_____

_____

_____

These are the things I like about myself:

These are the doubts I have:

8. I worry that if I begin to date, will I forget my spouse or, that I won't forget my spouse and anyone I date will be different than my partner. I know I should not compare and that might be a natural response to do but I am mindful of the fact that there are no replacements, and each person has his/her own merit. I will value each person for who they are -- knowing that they are different. I will recognize that I might have the tendency to compare but I will have the following attitude about dating:

_____

_____

_____

_____

_____

_____

_____

_____

_____

_____

_____

_____

_____

_____

_____

_____

_____

_____

_____

9. I will be open to explore new relationships without judgment, I will be mindful of:

_____

_____

_____

_____

_____

_____

_____

_____

_____

_____

_____

_____

_____

_____

_____

_____

_____

_____

_____

_____

_____

_____

_____

_____

_____

_____

10. I will trust myself in the following ways:

_____

_____

_____

_____

_____

_____

_____

_____

_____

_____

_____

_____

_____

_____

_____

_____

_____

_____

_____

_____

_____

_____

_____

_____

_____

11. Why am I still troubled by uncertainty? When a relationship is interrupted by loss, we are uncertain, uncertain of our future and our present. The past is uncomfortably gone. Taking one day at a time is helpful. *I will take one day at a time by:*

_____

_____

_____

_____

_____

_____

_____

_____

_____

_____

_____

_____

_____

_____

_____

_____

_____

_____

_____

_____

_____

_____

_____

12. I recognize I want to heal but sometimes I am still stumbling. I want to progress. When I am moving forward, these are the things I notice about myself:

_____

_____

_____

_____

_____

_____

_____

_____

_____

_____

_____

_____

_____

_____

_____

_____

_____

_____

_____

_____

_____

_____

_____

_____

_____

_____

13. I am excited about my good days. I am moving forward more than I am moving backwards. When I progress, these are the things I like about myself:

_____

_____

_____

_____

_____

_____

_____

_____

_____

_____

_____

_____

_____

_____

_____

_____

_____

_____

_____

_____

_____

_____

_____

_____

14. I am proud of myself because:

_____

_____

_____

_____

_____

_____

_____

_____

_____

_____

_____

_____

_____

_____

_____

_____

_____

_____

_____

_____

_____

_____

_____

_____

_____

4.

Time Sequence Four
Months Thirteen through Seventeen
Depression

The veil has lifted and you are no longer protected by shock; it is normal to experience some depression at this point. Much of the "busy work" has been resolved, creating time to finally process feelings.

For many people, successfully navigating the second year of mourning is more painful than the first. In the beginning, the psyche is protected. In the beginning, the emotions are frozen, but as time goes on, you will begin to defrost emotionally. It seems to be nature's way of protecting you. As the emotions return, the sadness is experienced on the deepest level, replacing the initial impact of loss and devastation.

However, despite the pain, there is significant growth in a forward movement as you begin to adapt to being alone. There is a back and forth nature to mourning. The range of emotions in the course of one day may vary quite a bit. You may wake up depressed, and then, as the day progresses, feel better. Or, you may feel happy in the morning and then be triggered by something in the course of the day and feel depressed. This is a normal response.

Triggers may be memories, dreams, music, photographs, movies, family events and holidays. Like a child learning to walk you might take one step forward, then fall, then pick yourself up and go forward again, each time getting stronger and gaining more confidence in your ability.

Another issue that continues to come up during this time is, "Is this all there is?" and "Am I going to spend the rest of my life lonely?" while, at the same time, you have been able to explore and experiment in new areas as you healed from the inside out. The layers of wounding take time to heal and the process cannot be rushed. People have their own timetables; simply put, it takes as long as it takes. Questions arise, such as, "When should I take off my wedding ring?

Anger turned inward also becomes depression. Depression often manifests itself as feelings of helplessness and being overwhelmed. It is the result of dealing with a new and unwanted life-change and expecting yourself to manage your daily obligations and emotions as you did when your loved one was alive. Seek help where and when needed and acknowledge every success, no matter how small. When the depression is not dealt with, the grieving process is delayed. Often it is helpful to speak with a therapist or counselor for assistance in dealing with these overwhelming feelings.

What does depression feel like? When you wake up in the morning you feel as if you are under a grey cloud. Lacking in motivation, you may move from one project to another, not completing any. The world looks weary. You sometimes feel hopeless, teary, and sad. You often feel tired. It is difficult to jump-start yourself out of bed; the covers look and feel good, it would be nice to linger for awhile. You don't see the light at the end of the tunnel. You cry easily or you feel locked up inside and can't cry at all. You eat too much to fill up the empty void or you can't eat at all, you have lost my appetite. You can fall asleep, but wake up within a few hours. You can't relax enough to fall asleep, the nights are very long. You may feel overwhelmed within yourself and not know where to turn for relief. You question: where am I and where am I going?

Libido? You're not sure that you have any anymore. Your energy for life is also low. You don't know how to put yourself back together. You often feel like humpty-dumpty having fallen off the wall. Will it get better? Will you be able to survive this?

1. When I feel the black cloud coming, I prepare for it by:

_____

_____

_____

_____

_____

_____

_____

_____

_____

_____

_____

_____

_____

_____

_____

_____

_____

_____

_____

_____

_____

_____

_____

_____

_____

_____

_____

_____

_____

2. I exercise even when I don't feel like it. I walk _____
miles per day, I swim, I stretch, I take an exercise class.
I will do more than think about it, I will MOVE and if I
move I will THINK less about myself and my troubles.
When I get weary I feel:

_____

_____

_____

_____

_____

_____

_____

_____

_____

_____

_____

_____

_____

_____

_____

_____

_____

_____

_____

_____

_____

_____

_____

_____

_____

3. I don't know what the rest of my life will be like but I can have a lot of influence on TODAY. This is what I will do TODAY to help myself:

_____

_____

_____

_____

_____

_____

_____

_____

_____

_____

_____

_____

_____

_____

_____

_____

_____

_____

_____

_____

_____

_____

_____

_____

_____

_____

4. I don't know if I will ever have romantic love in my life again, but I will not sit around idle. When I have healed enough, I will explore a social world by:

_____
_____
_____
_____
_____
_____
_____
_____
_____
_____
_____
_____
_____
_____
_____
_____
_____
_____
_____
_____
_____
_____
_____
_____

5. Long term goals are too far away. I will set a few short term goals for myself. The first goal I will set is:

_____

_____

_____

_____

_____

_____

_____

_____

_____

_____

The first step I will take in that direction is:

_____

_____

_____

_____

_____

_____

_____

_____

_____

_____

_____

_____

6. *I worry abut how I will live the rest of my life if I don't reconnect. I will take one step at a time, live in the now and make a commitment to living with less fear. When I get frightened or anxious I will accept that feeling about myself and release it. I will make an effort not to accelerate the fear or anxiety by dwelling on it. I will stay in the NOW and make plans for the NOW. I will be positive in my thinking by focusing on what I can do today. Today I will:*

_____

_____

_____

_____

_____

_____

_____

_____

_____

_____

_____

_____

_____

_____

_____

_____

_____

_____

_____

7. When I feel too much stress I will meditate by clearing my mind of the busy chatter. I will do this by breathing slowly. If my mind wanders, I will come back to paying attention to my breath; following the gentle inhale and exhale. I will concentrate on breath and only breath. I will relieve myself of too much thinking. I will start to do this today and practice daily. I will make time for meditation and/or relaxation. I can use relaxation tapes. I will commit to <u>allowing</u> myself to relax. I know I need to <u>allow</u> myself to relax; I cannot force myself to relax. This is how I am doing:

_____

_____

_____

_____

_____

_____

_____

_____

_____

This is where I would like to see myself:

_____

_____

_____

_____

_____

_____

_____

_____

8. When I am experiencing too much stress, I can use visual images to help me. I can use the image of the beach or a favorite vacation spot. In my mind's eye, I can go to this place fully with my visual skills, auditory, tactile, taste and smell. I can be fully there in this moment. I can begin my journey by finding that special place or places where I have experienced relaxation. I have been to the mountains or the beach. I know what it is like. I will go there now fully. Stretch on the sand, feel the pebbles and shells, feel the wind around my face, smell the salt air, and see the tall palm trees blowing in the wind. I will do this now and this is my experience:

_____

_____

_____

_____

_____

_____

_____

*This is how I feel after I have done this for 10-15 minutes:*_____

_____

_____

_____

_____

_____

_____

_____

_____

9. On the days I feel overwhelmed, what strategies should I employ? I will think; what am I overwhelmed about:

_____

_____

_____

_____

_____

What stresses can I reduce?

_____

_____

_____

_____

_____

How will I reduce them?

_____

_____

_____

_____

What can I take off my plate or if I have too many projects on too many burners, what can I remove?

_____

_____

_____

_____

_____

*10. I moved from my parents' home to a marriage. I now have to do everything by myself and I don't know how. When I am at a loss I will reach out to experts who know more than I do and I will learn. I will call the accountant, or my stock broker or my lawyer. I will question until I understand. I will call upon experts who know more than I do to educate myself. I may have children who have expertise; I will listen and wade through, not overwhelm myself but get educated. This is how I will **start** the process:*

_____

_____

_____

_____

I will not do this all in one day. I will go slowly so as not to be overwhelmed. This is what I have learned about myself:

_____

_____

_____

_____

_____

This is how I feel about myself as I am learning:

_____

_____

_____

11. How do I help myself get energy? When I am low on energy I notice the following things about myself:

_____

_____

_____

_____

_____

_____

_____

_____

_____

_____

_____

_____

_____

_____

_____

_____

_____

_____

_____

_____

_____

_____

_____

_____

*12. I know that in bereavement I can feel very drained and lethargic. I will boost myself by eating nourishing and appropriately healthy foods. I will eat lots of fruits and vegetables and stay away from fast foods and empty calories. I know that it is a very hard transition to shop and cook for one when I am used to doing it for two. However, I will make the effort to stay healthy because **I AM** important. I will do the following things for myself:*

_____

_____

_____

_____

_____

_____

_____

_____

This is how I feel about myself when I nurture myself properly:

_____

_____

_____

_____

_____

_____

_____

_____

_____

_____

13. I am used to having exercise in my life. I will continue to do the following things regularly:

_____

_____

_____

_____

_____

_____

_____

_____

_____

_____

_____

_____

_____

_____

_____

_____

_____

_____

_____

_____

_____

_____

_____

_____

_____

14. How do I get to feel hopeful that life will hold promise? I will encourage myself day to day. I will not go too far in advance because that will scare me. I will not tell myself scary stories. I will be hopeful one day at a time by using self-talk, positive affirmations and positive thinking. When I get into a negative cycle, I will reframe it. I will tell myself things like: I don't like this but I can do it. I will wash away the negative thought and replace it with a positive thought. I will "own" it, feel it and release it to the universe, replacing it with a calm and serene feeling. This is how I do it:

_____

_____

_____

_____

_____

_____

_____

This is how I feel about it:

_____

_____

_____

_____

_____

_____

_____

_____

_____

15. What part do I have to play in making life better? I have to play a major part. I have to work with myself. There isn't any "magic pill" or anyone else who can do it for me. I can receive support, guidance and wisdom from others but I must not forget to integrate the wisdom, support and guidance from myself. I have a lot to contribute to helping myself get better. When I talk to myself in a positive way, I say the following things:

_____

_____

_____

_____

_____

_____

_____

_____

_____

_____

_____

_____

_____

_____

_____

_____

_____

_____

_____

_____

_____

_____

16. I purposely try to encourage myself by:

_____

_____

_____

_____

_____

_____

_____

_____

_____

_____

_____

_____

_____

_____

_____

_____

_____

_____

_____

_____

_____

_____

_____

_____

_____

_____

_____

_____

_____

_____

_____

_____

17. When I am at a loss, I write in my workbook. When I release my feelings, then I feel:

_____

_____

_____

_____

_____

_____

_____

_____

_____

_____

_____

_____

_____

_____

_____

_____

_____

_____

_____

_____

_____

_____

_____

_____

_____

_____

_____

_____

18. I have a commitment to myself to gradually do better and I believe that I can. When I think about the positive things I can contribute, I feel:

_____

_____

_____

_____

_____

_____

_____

_____

_____

_____

_____

_____

_____

_____

_____

_____

_____

_____

_____

_____

_____

_____

5.

Time Sequence Five
Months Eighteen through Twenty Four
Integration, Adjustment, Transition

IT IS TIME TO successfully re-enter the world. Not the way it was but the way you now want it to be, with a new partner or not.

The final stage of grieving is integration, adjustment and transition. You make an "adjustment" in your life, a "transition" to the single world, and "integrate" the loss into your life while making positive steps to move forward.

How will you know when you are healing? This is when you can think of your loved one without strong emotional feelings of longing and sadness. You will remember him/her more realistically, neither as an idealized saint nor as a villain. You will be living in the present, not stuck in the past, and making plans for the future. Making peace with the loss implies moving forward, the pain and loss have lessened, and you are freer to move on with your own life.

In the final stage of grief, however, you may be surprised that you still experience some degree of depression. There is a lot of movement forward and sometimes backwards, which is all normal. "Is that all there is? Is this the rest of my life?" may still come up for you. Taking responsibility for one's life is not an easy thing; taking emotional charge of ones life is difficult. But to not take responsibility is to cause stress, to not make decisions causes stress, to sit in limbo causes stress.

You have worked through most of the grief issues and must now learn how to move forward productively with new friends, perhaps a new job, a new attitude, a new social life, or feel very stagnated. But hope is on the horizon when you make a commitment to your own growth, although you might still experience sadness and loneliness around special events (anniversaries, birthdays, and holidays). Or, you might feel stuck and need to revisit and resolve an earlier phase of grief.

An issue common to this time is: "Am I ready to start a relationship?" You might feel it is time because you are lonely and want to share your life with someone. Or you might feel scared because you feel "out of practice," fear rejection and may not be able to update your dating standards to fit into today's social world. Feelings of betrayal and guilt are still commonly felt when wanting to date.

You might feel that old friends find you a threat, and experience awkwardness; you don't know what to say around old friends. Old friends may identify with the deceased spouse and their own mortality causes them to retreat. Widows often feel like a "5th wheel" in a group with issues like who pays for dinner or theatre, causing everyone to be uncomfortable. You might even have dropped out of your married friends' lives because it is too painful and there are too many memories. Some widows handle this by inviting their married friends to dinner as a way of reciprocating the dinner invitations.

In new relationships, invariably what come up are possessions. For example: in taking on a new relationship, you might wonder how to blend what you own with what the new partner has. "If I move into his house, what do I do with what I have?" Deleting, discarding, sorting and throwing out become tasks of utmost importance and pain; associations resurface and memories of events associated with objects flood back. The reality is that by taking on a new relationship, you will give up some of the past in order to emerge beyond it. Also, by discarding and purging objects, you free up space for your new life which can be a cleansing process that provides relief, feeling freer and less attached to material objects.

Most importantly, you are ready to actively build a continuing life, where joys and pleasures can be experienced once again.

1. Why am I still having 'bad times' after being widowed for eighteen months? Bad times don't go away instantly. Some days are good and some days are mediocre. Eighteen months isn't magical. Some parts of days are good and some parts of days are moody and sad. Some days, you actually can enjoy yourself. But during the hard times, *these are the things I can do for myself to help me feel better about myself:*

_____

_____

_____

_____

_____

_____

I know that 18 months isn't any more magical than 24 months. I know I will have up and down days, but I will pay attention to caring for myself in the following ways:

_____

_____

_____

_____

_____

_____

When I need support I will:

_____

_____

_____

_____

2. Why did I think that after two years I would feel better? Two years is not a magical time frame. Freud said in 1909, that it takes a year and a half to two years to do the "work" of mourning, and indeed it is hard work. You move ahead to move back. Even though a support group may end at two years, you still continue to work through issues. However, by then most of the major tasks have been worked on. *When I get "stuck" I begin to look at the blessings in my life, they are the following:*

_____

_____

_____

_____

_____

_____

_____

_____

_____

_____

I am grateful for:

_____

_____

_____

_____

_____

_____

_____

_____

3. I do feel better, but some days I slip back, is that OK?. It is normal to go back and forth.

It is normal to do well and then not do well. The back and forth process is typical of a bereavement response. *When I slip back it is good for me to remind myself that this is normal. I will take care of myself in the following ways:*

_____
_____
_____
_____
_____
_____
_____
_____
_____
_____
_____
_____
_____
_____
_____
_____
_____
_____
_____
_____
_____
_____
_____

4. Some of my married friends now ignore me. It's hard for me to judge if they ignore me because they feel awkward around me, they've gone back to their own social life in a coupled world or they felt like they've done their good deed right after my husband/wife died. I am disappointed but I also recognize that I have to move on and develop a social network of my own. I will start that journey by:

_____

_____

_____

_____

_____

_____

_____

_____

_____

_____

_____

_____

_____

_____

_____

_____

_____

_____

_____

_____

_____

5. *Do I remind my married friends of their own vulnerability and their own mortality? Death often brings up fear in others ... that this "illness" will be catching. I am a reminder that they may lose their spouse. Instead of being disappointed, I will work with it in the following ways: I will talk to myself and, this is what I will say:*

_____

_____

_____

_____

_____

_____

_____

_____

_____

_____

_____

_____

_____

_____

_____

_____

_____

_____

_____

_____

_____

I will employ positive thinking and I will begin to build my single network in the following ways:

_____

_____

_____

_____

_____

_____

_____

_____

_____

_____

_____

_____

_____

_____

_____

_____

_____

_____

_____

_____

_____

_____

_____

_____

6. I feel resentful sometimes that my married friends have each other and I don't have my partner. Is that normal? It is totally normal to feel resentful. The question is what to do about it. It is OK to recognize your feelings and then make choices that work for you. *I don't have my partner. I can choose to be very unhappy and dwell on that or I can choose to open up my world and participate in activities I enjoy or want to learn more about. This is what I will do:*

_____

_____

_____

_____

_____

_____

_____

_____

_____

_____

_____

_____

_____

_____

_____

_____

_____

_____

_____

_____

7. How do I get out of myself and seek the larger world? When my world is too small I can't see past myself. I can't see beyond my own immediate pain and feelings. In order to open up my world I will participate in new activities, I will join activities that I have always wanted to and didn't have time for, I will actively seek new interests that excite me. I will give myself permission to explore new avenues. I will begin by:

_____

_____

_____

_____

_____

_____

_____

_____

_____

_____

_____

_____

_____

_____

_____

_____

_____

_____

_____

_____

_____

8. How do I find things to interest me when I get bored? If I am bored, it can be some depression, and lack of motivation which results in my not wanting to involve myself in the world. If I am bored I can go out of my way to explore, research, and try new behavior. I have to work with my own attitude. I will do that in the following ways:

_____

_____

_____

_____

_____

_____

_____

_____

_____

_____

_____

_____

_____

_____

_____

_____

_____

_____

_____

_____

_____

_____

9. How do I get out of my own emotionally stuck places? Do I recognize that I am stuck? If I am stuck, I will begin by recognizing that about myself. I will accept that and release it. I wish to move forward and I will do so in the following ways:

_____

_____

_____

_____

_____

By keeping stuck, I am perpetuating the following myths about myself:

_____

_____

_____

_____

_____

What do I gain by staying stuck:

_____

_____

_____

_____

_____

I will willing to try new things and learn new skills. I am willing to work with myself in the following ways:

_____

_____

_____

_____

10. How do I encourage myself to go forward? At a time in my life that I have low energy, I will recognize that I sometimes lack motivation. Instead of pushing myself, I will accept that about myself. At the same time, day by day, I will step forward to make progress by working with my attitude. I will list ten affirmations that are positive about myself:

1._____

_____

_____

_____

2.

_____

_____

_____

3.

_____

_____

_____

4.

_____

_____

_____

5.

_____

_____

_____

6.

_____

_____

_____

7.

_____

_____

_____

8.

_____

_____

_____

9.

_____

_____

_____

10.

_____

_____

_____

You have worked very, very hard to move through loss
to life and laughter. **CONGRATULATIONS!**

Bibliography

Albom, Mitch, <u>Tuesdays With Morrie</u>, Doubleday, 1997

American Association of Retired Persons, <u>On Being Alone</u>, 1909 K Street, N.W.

Washington D.C. 20049.

Ascher, Barbara Lazear, <u>Landscape without Gravity</u>, Penguin Books, NY, 1993

Beisser, Dr. Arnold, <u>Flying Without Wings: Personal Reflections on Loss, Disibility, and Healing</u>, Bantam Books, NY, 1988

Berkus, Rusty, <u>Life is a Gift</u>, Red Rose Press, Encino, CA. 1986

Bowlby, John, "Processes of Mourning" in <u>Grief: Selected Readings</u>, ed. Arthur C. Carr, et al. New York: Health Sciences Publishing, 1975, p. 13

Bozarth, Alla Renee, <u>Life Is Goodbye, Life Is Hello: Grieving Well Through All Kinds of Loss</u>, CompCare Publishers, Minneapolis, MN, 1982

Brabant, Sarah, <u>Mending the Torn Fabric: For Those Who Grieve and Those Who Want to Help Them</u>, Baywood Publishing Co., Amityville, New York, 1996

Brothers, Joyce, <u>Widowed</u>, Simon and Schuster, New York, NY, 1990.

Caine, Lynn, <u>Widow</u>, William Morrow and Co., 1974

Caine, Lynn, <u>Being a Widow</u>, Penguin Books, 1988.

Colgrove, Melba, <u>How to Survive the Loss of a Love</u>, Prelude Press, Los Angeles, CA, 1993.

Fisher, Ida and Lane, Byron, <u>The Widow's Guide to Life</u>, Prentice-Hall, Inc. Englewood Cliffs, New Jersey, 1981.

Gates, Philomene, <u>Suddenly Alone</u>, Harper, 1990

Ginsburg, Genevieve, Davis, <u>To Live Again</u>, St. Martin's Press, New York, NY, 1987

Ginsburg, Genevieve, Davis, <u>When You've Become a Widow: A Compassionate Guide to Rebuilding Your Life</u>, Tarcher, Los Angeles, 1987

Graves, Sandra L. & Shaw, Eva, <u>What To Do When A Loved One Dies</u>, Dickens Press

Grollman, Earl, A., <u>Living When a Loved One Has Died</u>, Beacon Press, Boston, Mass. 1977

Grollman, Earl, A., <u>What Helped Me When My Loved One Died</u>, Beacon Press, Boston, Mass., 1981.

Grollman, Earl, A., <u>Time Remembered: A Journal for Survivors</u>, Beacon Press, Boston, Mass., 1981.

<u>Healers On Healing</u>, Carlson, Richard & Shield, Benjamin, Editors, A. Jeremy T. Tarcher/Putnam Books, NY, 1989

James, John and Cherry Frank, <u>The Grief Recovery Handbook: A Step-by-Step Program for Loving Beyond Loss</u>, Harper and Row Publishers, New York, 1988.

Jewett, Claudia, L., Helping Children Cope With Separation and Loss, The Harvard Common Press, Harvard, Mass., 1982

Jewish Insights on Death and Mourning, Riemer, Jack, Editor, Schocken Books, NY, 1995

Klein, Melanie, quoted in Geoffrey Gorer, Death, Grief, and Mourning: A Study of Contemporary Society, Garden City, N.Y.: Doubleday and Co., Anchor Books, 1972.

Korn, Erroland Johnson, Karen, Visualization, The Use Of Imagery In The Health Professions, Dow Jones-Irvine, Homewood, Illinois, 1983, p. 32 (Holmes & Rahe) Stress Scale

Kramer, Herbert and Kay, Conversations at Midnight, William Morrow & Co., Inc. N.Y., 1993

Kubler-Ross, Elizabeth, On Death and Dying, Macmillan Publishing Co., Inc., New York, NY, 1969.

Kubler-Ross, Elizabeth, Death: The Final Stage of Growth, Prentice-Hall, Inc., Englewood Cliffs, New Jersey, 1975.

Lamm, Maurice, The Jewish Way in Death and Mourning, Jonathan David Publishers, New York, NY, 1969.

Leshan, Eda, Learning to Say Goodby, Avon Books, New York, NY, 1978

Levine, Stephen, Healing Into Life and Death, Anchor Books, Doubleday, NY, 1987

Levine, Stephen, <u>Who Dies?: An Investigation of Conscious Living and Conscious Dying</u>, Anchor Books/Doubleday, NY, 1982

Levy, Naomi, <u>To Begin Again</u>, Knopf, New York, 1999

Lewis, C.S., <u>A Grief Observed</u>, Harper, San Francisco, CA, 1994

Lord, Janet Harris, <u>No Time for Goodbye: Coping with Sorrow, Anger & Injustice After a Tragic Death</u>, Pathfinder Publishing, Ventura, CA, 1999

Lukas, Christopher, <u>Silent Grief: Living in the Wake of Suicide</u>, Charles Scribner's Sons, New York, NY, 1997

Manning, Doug, <u>Don't Take My Grief Away: What to Do When You Love a Loved One</u>, Harper and Row, New York, NY, 1984

Melges, Frederick, T. and Bowley, John, <u>Types of Hopelessness in Psychopathological Process</u>, Archives of General Psychiatry 20, 1969: 693-94.

Neeld, Elizabeth, <u>Seven Choices: Taking the Steps to a New Life After Losing Someone You Love</u>, Mira Bennett, Inc., Houston, TX, 1998

O'Connor, Nancy, <u>Letting Go With Love</u>, Bantam Books, New York, 1984

Olitzky, Kerris, <u>Grief In Our Seasons</u>, Jewish Lights Publishing, Woodstock, VT., 1998

Patterson, C.H., Relationship Counseling and Psychotherapy, Harper and Row Publishers, New York, NY, 1974.

Peck, Rosalie, Learning to Say Goodbye, Accelerated Development

Price, Eugenia, Getting Through The Night, Ballantine Books

Rando, Therese A., How to Go On Living When Someone You Love Dies, Bantam Double Day Dell, New York, NY, 1991

Schiff, Harriet, Sarnoff, The Bereaved Parent, Crown Publishers, 1977.

Simos, Bertha, G., A Time to Grieve, Family Service Association of America, New York, NY, 1979.

Sims, Darcie D., Why Are The Casseroles Always Tuna?, Big A & Co.

Staudacher, Carol, A Time To Grieve: Meditations for Healing After the Death of a Loved One, Harper, San Francisco, 1974

Tatelbaum, Judy, The Courage to Grieve, Family Service Association of America, New York, 1979

Thurman, Robert, The Tibetan Book of the Dead (Mystical Classics of the World) Bantam , NY, 1993

Truman, Jill, Letter To My Husband: Notes About Mourning and Recovery, Viking, 1987

Westberg, Granger E., Good Grief: A Constructive Approach To The Problem Of Loss, Augsburg Fortress, Minneapolis, MN, 1962

Williams, Colgrove, Bloomfield, How to Survive the Loss of a Love, Bantam, New York, NY, 1984.

Wolfelt, Alan D., Understanding Grief: Healping Yourself Heal, Accelerated Development Publishers, Philadelphia, PA, 1992

Wolfson, Dr. Ron, A Time to Mourn A Time to Comfort, The Federation of Jewish Men's Clubs, NY, 1993

Wolpe, David, Making Loss Matter, Riverhead Books, NY, 1999

Worden, J. William, Grief Counseling and Grief Therapy, Springer Publishing Company, New York, NY, 1982.

Yalom, I.D., The Theory and Practice of Group Psychotherapy, 2nd Edit., Basic Books, Inc., Publishers, New York, NY, 1975.

Zonnebelt-Smeege, Susan J., Getting to the Other Side of Grief: Overcoming the Loss of a Spouse, Baker Books, Grand Rapids, MI, 1998

Appendix A

Marilyn Stolzman, Ph.D., Executive Director
of H.O.P.E. Unit Foundation for Bereavement, Loss and
Transition

WHAT IS HEALING, and how do people heal? Seeking answers, I went to visit Rabbi Harold Schulweis to discuss it with him. The Rabbi suggested a "healing service" on the following Friday evening. He envisioned a panel of bereavement specialists to discuss how people change. The reality is that when participants come to our support groups, suffering and in anguish, they hardly want to be there. They are hurting so much and are bewildered. What can we do for them? Our goal was to find answers, ways to help the bereaved to heal, during this discussion and "healing service" at the Valley Beth Shalom in Encino, CA.

When Rabbi Schulzis welcomed us into his "house," we immediately felt that we were, indeed, in his spiritual "home," and felt very welcome. We knew that this feeling would need to be translated into our bereavement support group, i.e., to welcome newcomers into our program with acceptance and love regardless of denomination. We needed to "take them where they are," in despair, and slowly offer hope in keeping with Rabbi David J. Wolpe's theory as explored his book, Making Loss Matter: Creating Meaning in Difficult Times (Riverhead Books): "Growth comes through pain. Without loss, one remains a child. My hardest struggle is the struggle for faith, which, of course, I am still in. It constantly needs to be answered. It's essentially the struggle between my head and my heart."

As a therapist, I often say that there is a lag time between what the head knows and the heart can implement. When we bypass information from our head and our heart, the body speaks.

How do I help people heal? Through love, acceptance, humor, listening, being attentive and being "in the moment." Being present is sometimes all I can offer. I will never forget one bereaved client who said, "Just stand by me." A healing gesture is often being a "witness" to someone else's pain, and often the bereaved have a need to tell their story *over and over* again. As they tell their story, the pain, is diminished. As therapists, we need to have the patience to listen. At a time when the bereaved is impatient, we need to be patient. Often, less is better than more. The real essence of healing has a heart of spirituality.

The H.O.P.E. Unit Foundation
for Bereavement, Loss and Transition

The H.O.P.E. Unit Foundation for Bereavement, Loss and Transition is the oldest and largest bereavement support program that exists in the greater Los Angeles area, serving the community since the 1970s. We are non-profit and non-denominational. We offer ten weekly community support groups for widow/widowers, a loss of loved one group, and a cancer support group.

The H.O.P.E. Unit Foundation for Bereavement, Loss and Transition stands for: Hope, Opportunities, Participation and Education. **Hope** is our intention for healing grief with respect for people's differences in spiritual beliefs. We provide **Opportunities** for people to grow and learn from each other. **Participation** in a healing group atmosphere creates greater self-awareness. **Education** informs people about their physiological responses to grief and gives them information about the five stages of loss.

H.O.P.E.'s mission is to help people whose lives have been touched by loss by providing group support, educational programs and information to help alleviate the burdens and aloneness that exist in bereavement and cancer. Our groups are led by a long-established team of experienced, licensed therapists who are required to have additional training beyond their credentials. The bereavement program is unique in that individuals are placed in a time-framed group according to their months of mourning. Each group is mixed in ages but people share the same period of mourning. This makes for a more effective group process.

Our society does not prepare us for loss and people become devastated and overwhelmed when faced with crisis and the resultant decision-making process. People feel bewildered and are anxious to have direction, support and help through these most difficult times. Unaddressed grief can result in serious illness. We have found that people who regularly attend our program connect with each other and are less likely to be negatively affected by grief. We are serving over three thousand people a year with varied economic resources. People as they get older are more in need of community support and are healthier when they feel less lonely and isolated. Grief is a human response to loss.

H.O.P.E. Unit Foundation for Bereavement, Loss and Transition offers weekly community support groups, utilizing the skills of professionally trained licensed therapists. These experienced therapists receive additional training in bereavement support by the H.O.P.E. Unit Foundation.

We offer a two-year program in small support group settings for the Widow/Widowers population. The unique feature of this program is that individuals who come to use our services are placed in groups arranged according to months of mourning. For example: Group 1 is for 1-4 months, Group 2 is for 5-7 months, Group 3 is for 8-11 months, Group 4 is for 12-16 months, and Group 5 is for 17-24 months. All groups are mixed in age but are joined by the commonality of a specific phase of mourning. The therapists gear their approach according to the issues of the time frame of the group. We offer a support group for Family Loss and two Alumni support groups.

Over the years, thousands of people have attended our valuable programs and referred their friends. We provide a safe, non-judgmental environment in which family and community can be strengthened. We have learned an important part of the healing process is witnessing another's loss, and hearing their story. Grief will affect everyone at some point in their lives, when grief is not dealt with fully it leads to isolation, loneliness and depression. We are dedicated to helping people create permanent changes in their lives so that they can return to life with a sense of joy and with hope for the future.

For further information please contact:
Marilyn Stolzman, Ph.D.
H.O.P.E. Unit Foundation for Bereavement, Loss and Transition
P.O. Box 8034
Calabasas, CA 91372-8034
(818)788-4673
Web site: www.hopeunit.org

Appendix B

Life Does Go On
Benedict Carey

Life does go on, and for many it's surprisingly sweet; Grief over a spouse's death can give way to a new sense of fulfillment, researches say. **Benedict Carey**

SOME PEOPLE FOLLOW their spouses right through to the next world, dying mere hours or days after their beloved. It is sometimes suggested that the cause of death was a broken heart.

But while many people view widowhood as the start of a prolonged period of grieving and suffering, social scientists are finding that, more often than not, just the opposite is true. Researchers are finding that many men and women who lose a spouse not only survive the loss but usually resume satisfying lives over time,

"You do feel like you're dying yourself, at first," said Helen Kane, 83, of Downey, who lost her husband, Austin, four years ago to cancer. "It kind of comes as a surprise when you don't."

In studies during the last few years, researchers have found that many widows and widowers show no signs of mental anguish or need for counseling. Some recently widowed men and women actually report being *more* satisfied with their lives than peers whose spouses are alive. And now social scientists are beginning to understand exactly how so many of them discover a renewed sense of self-assurance, after losing their spouses.

"We focused for so long on the negatives of widowhood that we weren't able to acknowledge that there might be something good to say about it," said Deborah Carr, a sociologist at Rutgers University in New Brunswick, N.J., who presented the new research on life satisfaction at a recent aging conference.

"It is amazing to me that in some cases married women reported lower satisfaction with their lives than those who'd lost a spouse just six months before," Carr said.

The new findings on widowhood spring from an analysis of in-depth interviews with 1,532 Detroit-area seniors conducted in the 1980s and 1990s, as part of a University of Michigan project called Changing Lives of Older Couples, or CLOC. During the investigation, 319 of the participants were widowed. For the first time, researchers had enough information to compare people's lives before and after a spouse's death, rather than relying on memories. Analyzing the interviews and surveys, they have found that personality traits and marital relations can help predict one's experience of widowhood, and provide clues to how people manage its aftermath of loss and uncertainty.

Even when it's long expected, the death of a spouse is an emotional earthquake that psychologists rate as one of life's most distressing events. Kane said she was "in real, physical, aching pain for about a year," after her husband died.

When Jim Shoop's wife died seven years ago, his days became "all blackness." As you grow older, said the 80-year-old Downey resident, "you find that your spouse is much closer to you than ever before, when both of you were working and raising kids. You're always together with this person, and then one day they're gone."

About a quarter of the Michigan widows and widowers reported serious depression after their spouses died. But George Bonanno, a psychologist at Columbia University in New York who studies grief and recovery, recently compared the interview responses more closely and found that nearly half of these people were depressed *before* their spouses died. "Losing a spouse undoubtedly *exacerbates* the depression in many cases," Bonanno said, "but it didn't *cause* it in these people."

Among those who did experience depression just after being widowed, Bonanno found high levels of a specific personality trait: an anxious neediness. In surveys taken before their spouses died, these husbands and wives tended to agree with statements such as, "I imagine the worst if a loved one doesn't arrive on time," and "People sometimes don't realize how easily they can hurt me." While such people are in the minority, they tend to be highly sensitive to being betrayed and have a preoccupation or fear of being abandoned, Bonanno said, adding that these people often require counseling.

By far the most common experience of grieving is what psychologists call the *resilient pattern*, an acceptance of death that gives way to recovery of energy and interest in beginning a new life. Sometimes this process can drag on for a year or more, complicated by squabbles over an estate, or lack thereof. But most often it happens within the first year after the death.

After her husband of 34 years, Judah, died of a viral infection last September, Alice Graubart, 57, a Chicago social worker, had nightmares almost every night. "I was reliving the circumstances of his death a lot – the hospital scenes, the way he looked. It was awful," she said. After three months, however, the anguish finally broke; the nightmares faded and a sense of normality returned. "It's a new normal," she said. "He's not here, but I feel like myself again."

One reason older adults recover more quickly is they've had more life experience, psychiatrists say. By age 60, most have had at least one parent, friend or family member die; they've had scares about high blood pressure, high cholesterol, polyps or cysts, and lived through the mid-life reckoning with their own mortality. "After a certain age, widowhood is not unexpected, it's almost a developmental milestone of late life, neither surprising nor abnormal," said Dr. Gary Kennedy, past president of the American Assn. for Geriatric Psychiatry. "This is not to say that it can't be devastating. But provided the person had a good marriage, there's a lot to be built upon."

Yet it's doing for oneself that helps people climb out of their misery, according to Carr, the Rutgers sociologist. In a new study of dependence and widowhood based on the Michigan data, Carr found that men who relied on their wives for tasks such as cooking, laundry and housework tend to report high levels of satisfaction when widowed. Some widowers find another woman to help look after them; but others find surprising pleasure in the small chores of daily living once done by their spouses. After coming to terms with the death of his wife, Claire, 14 years ago, Wilbur Yonan, 78, of Long Beach, discovered grocery shopping. "It's something I like to do now. I get a charge out of it, though I'm not sure most widowed men feel that way," said Yonan, who's now remarried.

Women who relied on their husbands for emotional support likewise reported high levels of life satisfaction in widowhood, the research suggests. Many of these women were in stifling relationships to start with, explains Carr, and probably were lacking in self-confidence while married. After losing a spouse, they find strength in simply living and providing for themselves, something they'd thought unimaginable before.

But there's more to this adjustment than simply escaping the manipulations of a demanding spouse. In almost any long marriage, Carr argues, there are parts of our personality that are put on hold or fall into the background of the relationship. "At some level in a long marriage, people forget about an aspect of themselves, something that wasn't fostered by their partner," she said. "In a sense you can lose some private part of yourself in a marriage that can now be rediscovered when you're alone. Sometimes you need a shock to make you see those things, and make a real change in your life."

Helen Kane rarely had to visit the post office, bank or cleaners because her husband took care of those chores during their marriage. "I would think nothing of saying, 'Oh, stop and get stamps', or, 'Go ahead and drop this off at the bank,' and that was that," she said. "I really never made those trips myself." Since he died, she has little choice.

A hospice volunteer who also counsels other widows, Kane said one of the first tests of a newly widowed person's emotional resilience comes in April—tax month. "For people who never had to worry about the finances, it's a big deal to get that done, because you can't concentrate very well after this person has left you, and it's very hard to close out a year when you've got a death in it."

Over time, the oddest thing for many widows and widowers may be that the initial shock and grief soften, the waves of sadness no longer crash on every anniversary, and what was once such a painful and persistent event drops gradually into the past. It's as if the emotional chemistry has altered, which, psychologists now say, is normal.

For many years, said Columbia University's Bonanno, the common belief among mental health experts was that people who didn't continually grieve after the death of a spouse were unfeeling or in denial about unresolved issues. "But now we can say that this is how human-beings handle the loss of the most important person in their lives," he said. "They grieve and move on."

About the Authors

Gloria Lintermans

LOS ANGELES-BASED **Gloria Lintermans** is a widow, freelance writer and former internationally syndicated columnist; her column appeared in English and Spanish language newspapers across the U.S. from Hawaii to New York and worldwide from Saudi Arabia to South America.

Lintermans is the author of the enormously successful *CHEAP CHIC: A Guide to LA's Resale Boutiques* (1990), the "ultimate guide to recycled fashion," and forerunner of *RETRO CHIC: A Guide to Fabulous Vintage and Designer Resale Shopping in North America & Online* (Really Great Books, Los Angeles, 2002) and *The Newly Divorced Book of Protocol* (Barricade Books, New York, 1995). Lintermans has also written for numerous national and local magazines.

Lintermans has appeared on radio and television talk shows across the country including: the "Donna Mason Show," Raleigh, NC; "Steve Kalk Show," Beaver Falls, PA; "Morning Drive with John Dawson," Albany, GA; "Tim Quinn Show," Bridgeport, CT, "What You Should Know About," Philadelphia, PA; "Memphis in the Morning," Memphis, TN; "Kent Slocum Show," Grand Rapids, MI; "The Michael Jackson Show," Los Angeles, CA, among others. She has hosted her own "Looking Great with Gloria Lintermans" cable television and radio shows and is a popular lecturer and commentator.

Lintermans is a member of The Authors Guild, Inc., the National Society of Newspaper Columnists and A.F.T.R.A. (American Federation of Television & Radio Artists). Lintermans lives in Los Angeles.

Lintermans is a widow whose experience of loss and new love has become the basis for THE HEALING POWER OF GRIEF: The Journey from Loss to Life and Laughter and THE POWER OF LOVE: Transcending the Loss of a Spouse to New Romance.

Marilyn Stolzman

DRAWN TO THE healing aspect of grief counseling, Los Angeles-based **Dr. Marilyn Stolzman** became a professional counselor specializing in bereavement. After acquiring her hospice training, an internship at the American Cancer Society, and her L.M.F.T. license, Dr. Stolzman was hired and trained by the head of social services at Encino Hospital in Southern California to lead their hospital's bereavement program; at that point, she had been a practicing therapist for a year and had started a cancer support group for women in 1973 at the Mid-Westchester YWCA in Scarsdale, NY. Dr. Stolzman is a certified clinical Hypnotherapist and a Somatic Experiencing Practitioner. She has bee in private practice in Woodland Hills, California since 1981. She is a popular lecturer and has lectured for The American Institute of Medical Education in France, Hawaii, Santa Fe and Hong Kong. She has also been a frequent lecturer at The Oaks in Ojai, CA, Kaiser Permanente, and Pierce College, Woodland Hills, CA.

She has taught bereavement classes at the Phillips Graduate Institute in Southern California, and for doctorate students at Ryokan College in Venice, CA. She has taught Continuing Education classes at California State University Northridge and at Encino-Tarzana Regional Medical Center. She is completing a book on Hypnosis with colleague Trudy Moss, Ph.D.

Most recently, Dr. Stolzman directs the Southern California bereavement and transition support program, H.O.P.E. UNIT FOUNDATION, Bereavement, Loss and Transition, which offers a life-affirming two-year support group program. The literature supports that people do 50 percent better if they attend a bereavement group. It helps people to "normalize" feelings and receive validation and feedback from each other and from the therapists. People know they are not alone, not isolated. Group support makes people recognize that they are not going crazy. There is comfort in knowing that others feel the same way. Everyone goes through their grieving differently depending on their own ego strengths, their history, their coping strategies and their life experience. A support group needs to provide a safe, warm atmosphere where people can trust that what they share is contained and stays in the group. It is important for the group to be led by licensed professionals. This experience has become the basis for *THE HEALING POWER OF GRIEF: The Journey Through Loss to Life and Laughter* and *THE HEALING POWER OF LOVE: Transcending the Loss of a Spouse to New Love.*

To order online visit www.championpress.com

THE HEALING POWER OF LOVE:
Transcending the Loss of a Spouse to New Love
Gloria Lintermans & Marilyn Stolzman, Ph.D., L.M.F.T.

"To love is to receive a glimpse of heaven."
Karen Sunde

THE HEALING POWER OF LOVE: *Transcending the Loss of a Spouse to New Love* is a collection of twelve beautifully and honestly told, uplifting and inspirational stories of new, loving relationships following the loss of a spouse or partner. Of the books currently available, not one addresses the life-affirming, vitally important, next step following mourning the loss of a spouse or partner. The often disquieting yet exhilaratingly overlap of grieving <u>and</u> finding new love can only unfold through a commitment to healthy grieving and the willingness to move forward.

To love and be loved is to feel the sun from both sides.
David Viscott

THE HEALING POWER OF LOVE is presented in a simple format, one chapter for each of the twelve couples, yet the subject is complex, an emotionally charged, multi-layered one due to the often ongoing grief over the loss of a spouse while, at the same time, falling in love all over again. Chapter-by-chapter, twelve men and women, widows and widowers of all ages, from all walks of life and situations, share—in their own words— stories of their life-affirming, new loving relationships and the road they each traveled in order to realize them. Each of the twelve chapters begins with an introduction to the couple, a sharing of their experience, from both the male and female perspectives, and concludes with thought-provoking, comments from Marilyn Stolzman., Ph.D., L.M.F.T.

Each couple shares the following:
- The length of their marriage or partnership.
- Length of time since spouse or partner passed away.
- A description of the support offered by friends and family for their grieving.
- Whether a grief support group of counseling was attended and for how long.
- If so, how it helped each to heal their grief.
- During their first two years of mourning, what their hardest period of time was and why.
- At what point in the grieving each began to date.
- Did each begin dating because they were overcome with loneliness and lack of physical intimacy, or did each feel that they were ready to begin a deep friendship? How they met their current partner. Whether or not they were friends before becoming romantically involved.
- How their new relationship impacted their feelings for late spouse or partner.

- How this new person is different from their late spouse or partner. How this difference impacted their relationship.
- How scary it was to become emotionally vulnerable with this new person. How scary it was exploring physical intimacy again.
- How they dealt with today's expectations of sexuality and how it affected their performance. What their expectations were regarding sexual intimacy. Were they able to talk about these expectations with their new partner?
- What the bumps in-the-road were in this new relationship. What they wished they could have done differently.
- Trouble spots with family getting along with their new partner.
- The future they envision with this person.
- Advice for others in your circumstance.

Consider this brief excerpt from Gloria's story:

Moving from intellectual concept to emotional reality required such a giant leap of faith when the opportunity to become involved in a new relationship presented itself. Almost a year and a half after my husband died, I was finally doing great. I had a great career, good and loving friends and family. I had created a satisfying balance in my life. I was feeling good, strong and grateful for the joy that I was once again able to embrace. And then Hal came along.

I had moved beyond thinking that sex would again be part of my life, and that was fine, putting my creative energies into other aspects of my life. While the idea of perhaps loving someone again was always a possibility, it was only an intellectual exercise at that point. I knew that if it happened, ok, if not, my life was fully satisfying. Well, I was knocked for a loop. I was so attracted to Hal, emotionally, intellectually, and yes, physically. He wanted sex. I wanted a level of emotional comfort. Perhaps they're the same thing. Yet I struggled to keep my emotionally safe life intact.

Slowly I began to trust this relationship. Or, perhaps, better said, I began to trust myself to know what I wanted in a new relationship, and so, was able to meet him halfway. It's still scary, but my level of comfort is growing. But, the reality is that this relationship is understandably complicated by an elephant in the room – my feelings towards my late husband and my guilt. The reality is that this relationship has four people, two of which have a vote. Sometimes crowded, sometimes distracting,

He is a widower, with loving memories of his late wife. And that is good. But I may be further along in healing my grief over losing my late husband. I guess it comes down to this idea: Would I rather be an emotionally pampered widow, or a vulnerable newcomer to love? There is status in being the brave, resourceful widow that looked pain and loss in the eye and said, so what!"

Love is, above all else, the gift of oneself.
Jean Anouilh (1910 – 1987)

Authors **Gloria Lintermans and Marilyn Stolzman, Ph.D., L.M.F.T.** have come together once again to create this book after earning their bereavement accreditations and re-loving experience worlds apart—Dr. Stolzman by way of her professional training and work as a professional counselor specializing in bereavement and the Director of H.O.P.E. Unit Foundation for Bereavement, Loss and Transition, a non-profit organization sponsoring unique bereavement support groups for hundreds of people in Southern California, and Lintermans, who has mourned, healed and recovered following the death of her husband.

Together they explore and reveal the intricacies to creating new, loving relationships following the loss of a spouse. Lintermans is a former syndicated newspaper columnist, currently a freelance writer and author. She has also hosted her own cable television show and radio program. She is the author of *The Newly Divorced Book of Protocol* (Barricade Books, New York, 1995) and *Retro Chic* (Really Great Books, Los Angeles, 2002).

THE HEALING POWER OF LOVE embraces widows/widowers and life-partners, offering stories of hope for re-creating a life of joy, meaning, and fulfillment.

One word frees us of all the weight and pain of life: That word is love. Sophocles (496BC – 406 BC)